PRESENTED TO

_____

FROM

_____

DATE

_____

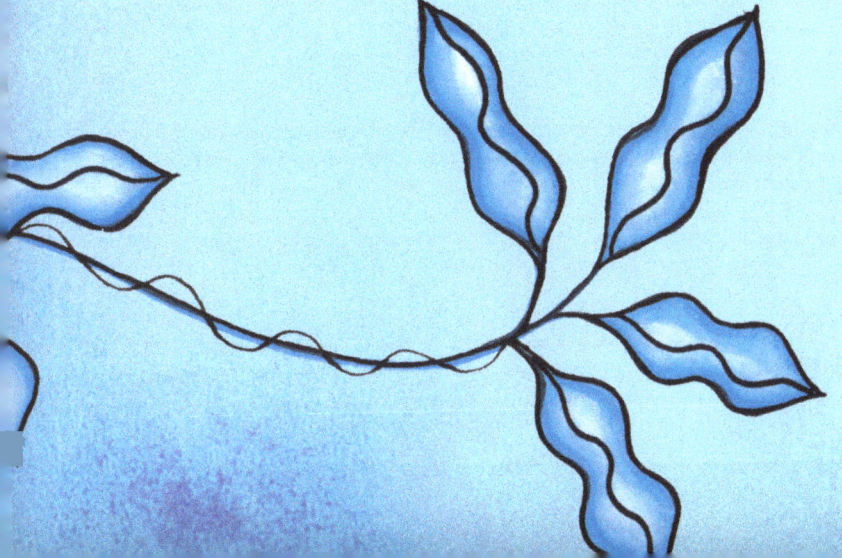

This book is dedicated to all my "Songbirds"—
my family, children, grandchildren and friends.
May you sing the song God has given you.

Songbird Inspired books may be purchased in bulk at special discounts for sales promotion, corporate gifts, fund-raising or educational purposes. Special editions can also be created to specifications. For details, contact the company via email at songbirdinspired@gmail.com

Unless otherwise noted, Scripture quotations are taken from the ESV© Bible (The Holy Bible, English Standard Version). Copyright ©2001 by Crossway, a publishing ministry of Good News Publishers. All rights reserved.

Illustration: Kadie Schaefer
Art Direction: Sara Lin

Library of Congress Control Number: 2025905583
ISBN: 979-8-9925756-2-0

TRACY FEDYSKI

Songbirds
Learn to
Sing in the
Dark

EXPERIENCING GOD THROUGH POETRY

Learning to
Hear God's Voice in the Dark

II

Emerging Out of Darkness and Singing in the Light

Foreword

"Tracy Fedyski's words do not merely rest on pages—they rise, resound, and sing. She invites the reader to lean in close and hear the whispers of God echoing through valleys, victories, and vulnerable spaces. Like the songbird trained in darkness to recognize its father's voice, Tracy teaches us how to wait, listen, and trust the holy hush that precedes the dawn.

Every poem hums with the healing cadence of a woman who has learned to let grief be a tutor and joy be her anthem. Through Tracy's gift, the Holy Spirit gets to hold the pen. The result? A chorus of truth, grace, and sacred encouragement. This is not just a book—it's a tender call back to the Voice that first spoke love into us.

So, if your heart has ever limped through the valley or longed for the morning, let *Songbird* be the lantern you carry. Tracy's song is strong, Spirit-led, and gently unforgettable."

—Cindy Goodman
Minister, Recovery Advocate,
and Fellow Songbird-in-Training

"Those among us who yearn to experience a dynamic relationship with God will cherish these new and fresh ways of communicating the melodies hidden in our hearts. In this beautiful book, Tracy freely and creatively shares with us how she experiences the Psalms and hymns and spiritual songs that characterize her daily walk with God. She is entrusting to us the very intimate heart of her personal relationship with her Creator."

—Holly DelHousaye
Author of From God's Heart, To My Pen
todayforeternity.com

"What is God teaching you in the valleys, the stillness, the darkness of the night that you can sing to others in the day? As Tracy's concept for this book began to unfold, I could tell it was going to be something like I have never read or experienced before. The depth, creativity, and genuine exploration of God's character and love come alive through the words so beautifully displayed in this book of poetry. Through Tracy's love and admiration for her Savior and His creation, she has given us a glimpse into what is possible for all who are willing to walk closely with our Creator, seeking to hear His voice above all else, so that we can then sing our song for others in the day!"

—Kadie Schaefer
Artist, Author, and Illustrator

"Have you learned to 'sing in the day, what you learned in the night'? Tracy Fedyski, has not only experientially learned, but she is also sharing in poetic 'psalm-like' words the 'life learnings' of her heart. These insights could only be learned from a close walk with her loving Father.

You will relate personally to this passionate, relationship-rich journey through the poetic realities of our Author. Her gift is to share this precious and personal learning journey with us, so that our songs may be filled with His joy, love, and grace. Enjoy every stanza, and share with family and friends."

—Naomi Rhode
Speaker, Author, Coach
CSP, CPAE Speaker Hall of Fame
Past President, National Speakers Association
Past President, Global Speakers Federation

Prologue

I will never forget the day when I was walking out of church and I heard a still, small voice say, "One day you will write a book." In my head I said, "Who, me? I am not a writer! I am just a girl who is in love with you, Jesus. YOU saved me out of my addiction and gave me new life! I now have a husband, two young children, and a thriving business to run." That voice who encouraged me to write a book one day ... never left me. I KNEW it was the voice of God. Year after year, I would ask the same question, "Is it time to write the book?" The answer was, "No ... not now."

I love to read and I remember reading about how songbirds learn to sing in the dark. They hear their father's voice at night and sing it in the day. This intrigued me so much and never left my mind. During this time of waiting on God's timing to write my book, He gave me amazing opportunities to foster my faith and grow in my passion for teaching, training, and leading Bible studies. I met people from all around the globe, of all ages and stages. I have spent over thirty-six years in church and marketplace ministry discipling others.

I now have six grandchildren and my hope is to pass on my passion for using the gifts God has given each of them. I remember the day many years later, God said, "Now it's time." "... Really? Now? Wow!" I began to write poetry, songs, and stories out of my own experiences with God in learning to hear His voice in the darkness, as I finally processed some grief and trauma in His presence. Emerging out of the dark and singing the songs in the light gives me great delight. God has allowed this ordinary girl to encounter Him, people, and places I never dreamt possible. My prayer is this book will foster growth in your faith to experience God in your darkness and see your valley differently.

If you are going through a valley, this is the time to listen to God, to be silent, and to obey your Father's voice. Remain quiet. The One who created you, the One who loves you, the One who has a plan and purpose for your life—He wants to speak to you. Be encouraged! The Lord has something to tell you. "Be still and know that I am God" (Psalm 46:10). In your darkest valley, listen and obey. It is a discipline, and when you emerge out of darkness, as the Songbird, you will have a beautiful song to sing—a message to sing in the light that God has given to you. You, my friend, are the Songbird.

This book of poetry holds within its pages my testimony of learning to hear God's voice in the dark, in the valleys of life, emerging out of darkness, and singing in the light. "Jesus told his disciples, 'What I tell you in the dark, say in the light, and what you hear whispered, proclaim on the housetops' (Matthew 10:27). The Lord showed me today that had I not gone through some major grief and sorrow the last several years, this book would have never come about the way it has—or should I say, perhaps I finally allowed myself to feel the pain and not find something else to numb it … or find another coping mechanism.

Allowing myself to heal with the help of God Almighty and a community of like-minded friends has given me freedom in Christ like I never thought possible.

This book was solely birthed out of my relationship with Jesus.

I hope it helps you in a relevant way.

The way it has helped me see my valley differently.

The way the Lord shows up in His masterful sovereignty.

The way God is with us in the dark.

The way Jesus speaks to us through His Word.

The way the Holy Spirit comforts us when we groan.

The way the valley prunes.

The way the sorrow hurts.

The way the grief takes its turn.

One day sad and one day mad.

One day acceptance.

The way of the valley has purpose.

The way of the valley has shown me

God's sovereignty,

His masterful sovereignty.

I see the valley so differently.

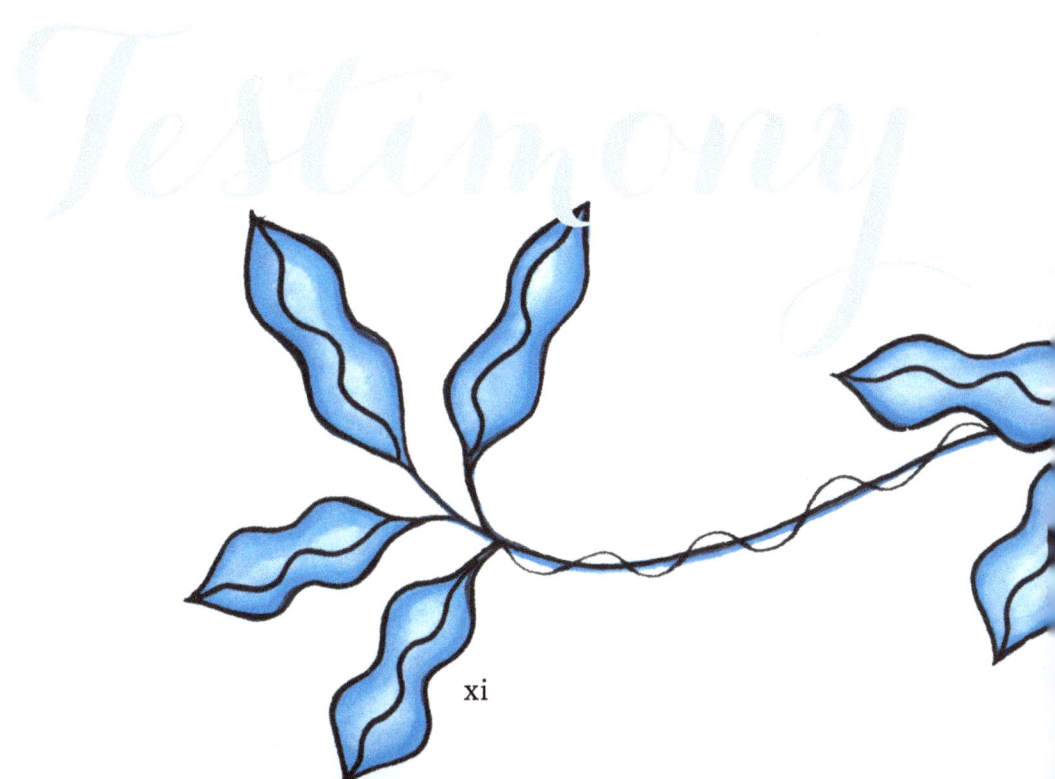

1

Learning to Hear God's Voice in the Dark

The Songbird Learns to Sing at Night

The songbird learns to sing at night

When all is still, silent, and without flight

He hears the song of his father's voice so sweet

In the darkness, he repeats

Over and over until just right

When all is still, silent, and without flight

The songbird learns to sing at night

His father's voice so sweet, a tune he can repeat

And when the time is just right

The morning comes—

The songbird takes flight

To sing his father's song by day

For all to hear so sweet

Because the songbird learned to hear his father's voice at night

When all was still, silent, and without flight

You, O Lord, are the song I want to sing

You give me Your melody

You give me Your Word for my soul

You give me Your grace when I am weak

You give me Your love that I don't even seek

You give me Your joy and strength

You, O Lord, are the song I want to sing

You give me the melody

Song of Beautiful

What a beautiful song you will sing

O Child of the King

When you hear your

Father's voice in your darkest moment

When the walls are closing in

There is nowhere else to turn

You are at the end of yourself

You in your own power

Have tried everything to cope—

Nothing helps the hurt

What seems to help at first

Turned to chains that bound you

Even more ...

That new relationship, those new clothes,

That vacation, that drink, that pill—

You fill in the blank

Oh, what a lure

To try try try

In your own strength

To fix or fill an old habit

Or wound

Or open sore

The Lord wants to speak to you in

Darkness through HIS Word

Through HIS still small voice

Through your circumstances you find yourself in

HIS voice is a salve to your wound

Only Jesus can heal your brokenness

So will you let Him in?

Receive Him as your Lord and Savior?

Let HIM take your darkness and turn it to

Light

Your broken life doesn't scare HIM

HE wants to speak life into your dark places

And then you will find your voice

The voice that finds

Purpose in your pain

Purpose in your suffering

Purpose in your failure

Purpose in your addiction

Purpose in your life!

You are the Songbird!

You are the Songbird!

What a beautiful song you will sing

O Child of the King

Sing your new song

O Child of the King

Sing your new song

O Child of the King!

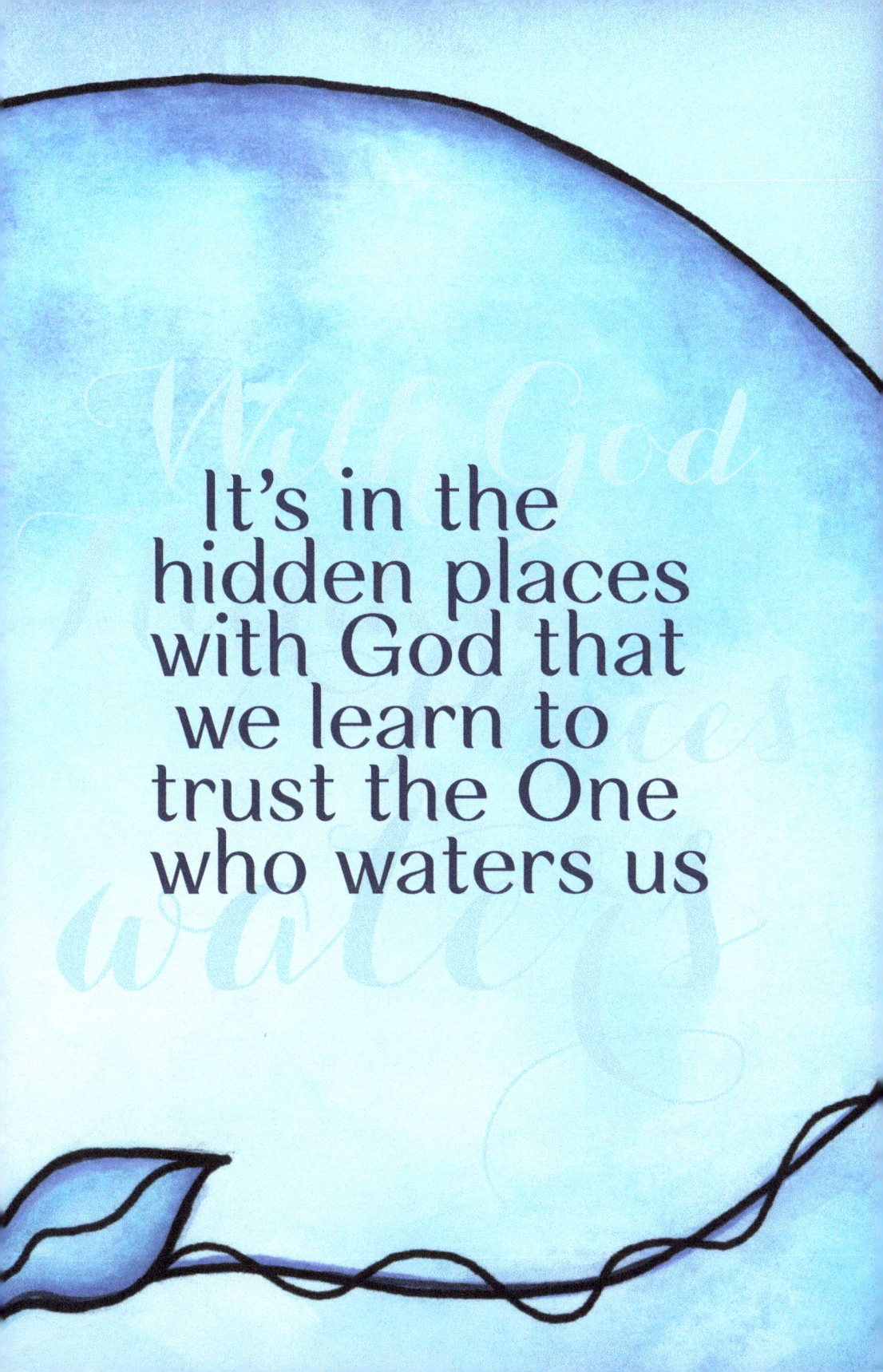

It's in the hidden places with God that we learn to trust the One who waters us

Song of Happy

I love sunflowers.

There is something about the vibrant color that contrasts with the blue sky.

They stand tall, waiting to say hello.

They are happy—I always
smile when I see one.

I've never met a sunflower I didn't like
or the Song of Happy they sing
to me.

I gave a loved one sunflower seeds to plant in their garden. The sunflowers are already growing very tall. There is something very special about watching something grow from seed. It takes the right soil, water, sun, and nurturing. I so appreciate nature and growth. There is so much done where we can't see. So I sing the Song of Happy.

Seeds are planted where

It's dark

This is where they

Begin to grow

Taking root in the

Hidden places

Where no one can see

It's like our faith rooted

In Christ Jesus

It first begins as a small

Seed planted

By the Word of God

Then it takes root in the

Hidden places

In our heart

Where only God can

See

The Word of God begins

To nourish our soul

It's in the hidden places with God

That we grow

And learn to

Trust

The One who waters us

Seeds are planted where it's

Dark

They are watered and nourished

And at the right time

They begin to sprout

It's in the hidden places

Where a lot of growth is done

For the root needs to be strong

It's in the hidden places with God

That our roots become strong

And when the time is just right

We begin to sprout in faith

There is something vibrant about

The one who spends

Time with God

Alone

Much like the sunflower

That blooms and follows the sun

It was in the hidden places

The flower learned to sing the Song of Happy

To give it away

As we look to the One who waters us

Nourishes us

And begins to prune us

It's in the hidden places with God

That we begin to see

The pruning is meant to be

It's where we truly

Learn the Song of Happy

There is something resilient

About the one who spends

Time in the hidden places

With God

They want to give their seeds away

Their seeds of faith

By the Word of God

So others can learn

The Song of Happy

Inspired by

John 15:2, Psalm 91

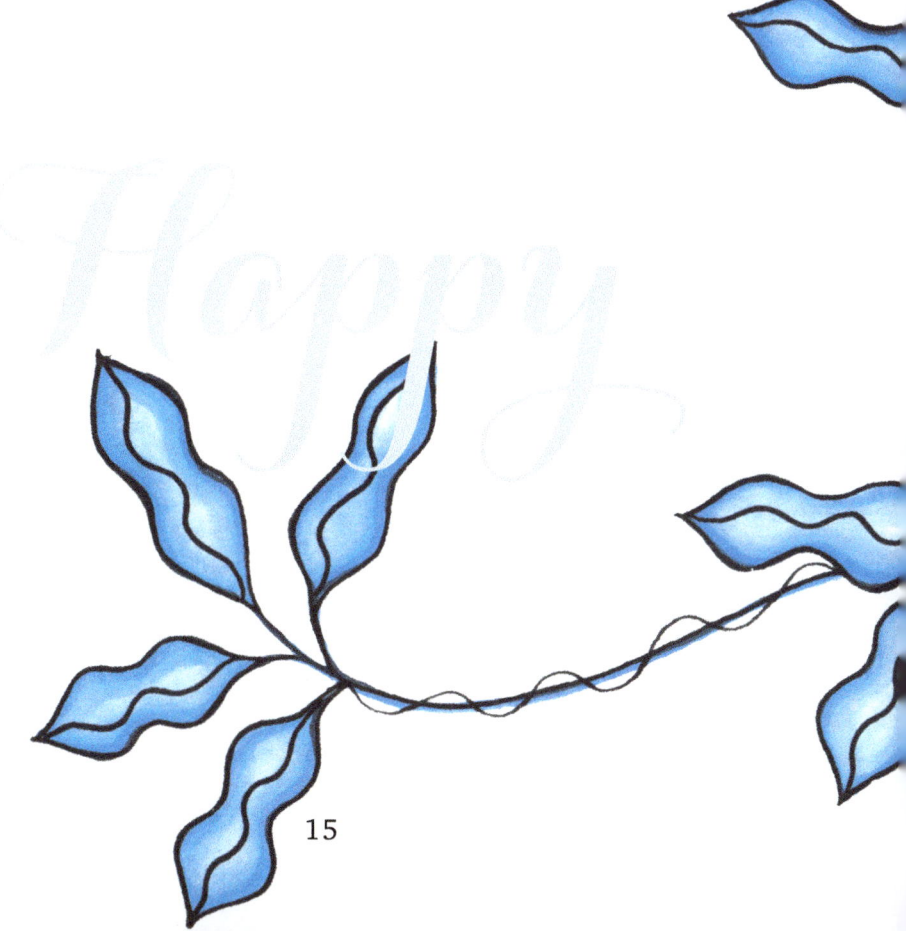

Song of Rain

When the summer rains make their way into

The Valley of the Sun

The desert begins to have a sweet smell

As the clouds begin to roll in

The storm is brewing

Thunder claps

Lightning dances in the sky

The desert is ready

For the summer rain

So sweet the smell

During these hot summer days

In the Valley of the Sun

The rain is a gift

The ground drinks it in

The mountains turn a shade of green

The cacti bloom

Shades of yellow, pink, and orange

The desert critters come out for a peek

During these hot summer days

The rain is a gift

We all drink it in

We all drink it in

There is something hard to explain

About the desert rain

It's like a drink from heaven

It's like a drink from heaven

Won't you drink it in?

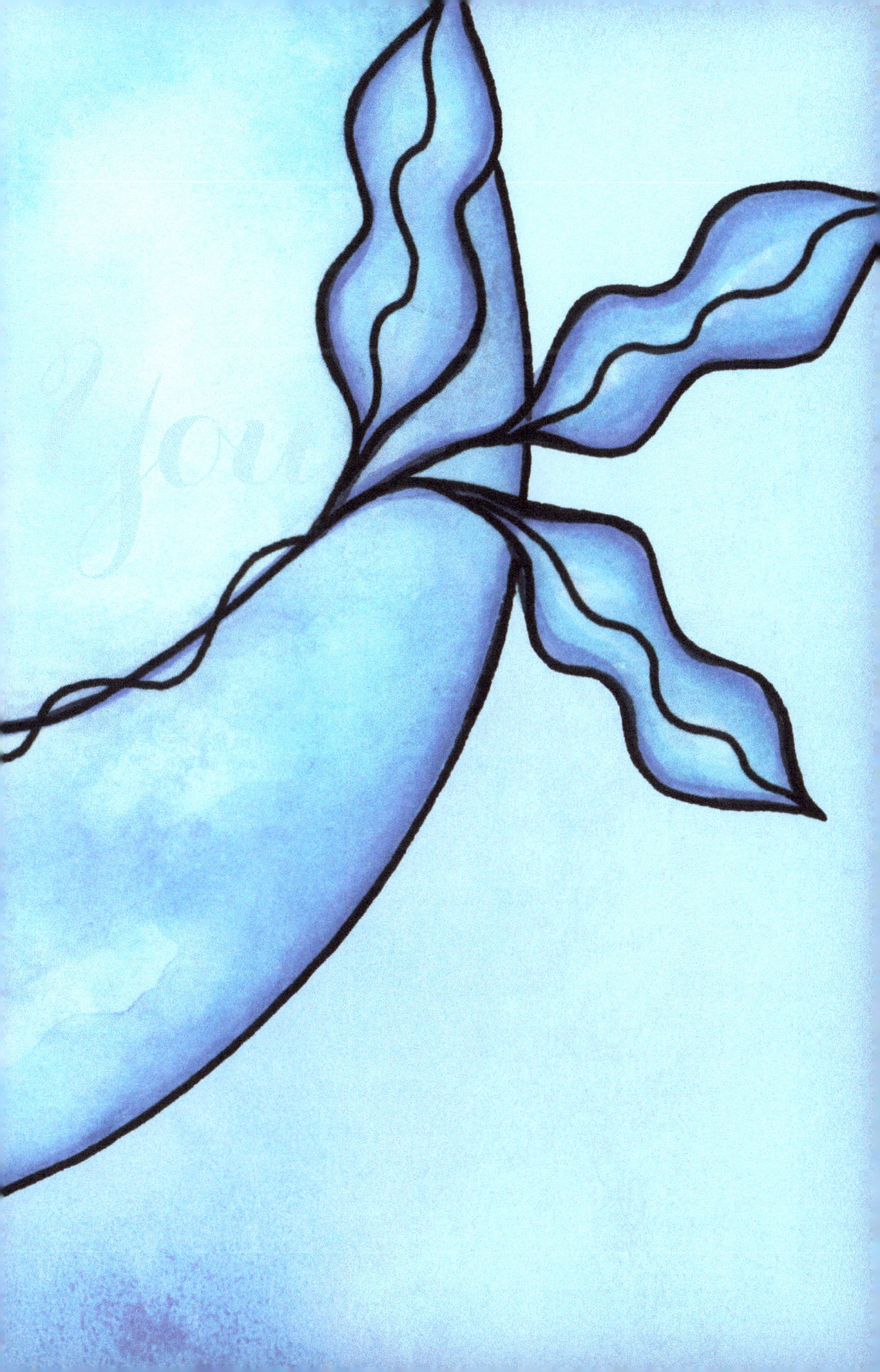

Song of the Shepherd

There is a ranch in Arizona that I love to wander around. When I enter the gates of this ranch, a peace will rush over me. Something about being in the presence of such beauty. The majestic silhouette of the horses amidst the blue Arizona sky with the mountains in the backdrop. It is a beauty to behold. It is like God is saying, "Look what I made just for you today!"

I had the privilege of teaching a Bible study on the ranch for a season. I would arrive early on occasion just so I could say "hello" to all the animals. The sheep and the desert tortoise, the potbellied pigs, the goats, and all their friends—the chickens and the hens.

When I would walk up to the fence, some of the horses would approach me with a friendly greeting. What I noticed most was their eyes. I felt like they could look into my soul. Just to be clear, I am not a cowgirl nor a rancher. God seems to put me in places I would never go myself, but when I listen to His voice,

His direction, His call …

and say yes …

I notice there is always something exciting up ahead.

I was at the ranch to lead a Bible study, but what I realize now is that God has purpose in His placement for a reason and a season, so I may experience God and His creation in a new way. So I sing the Song of the Shepherd.

The Shepherd has a voice

It is just for you

And it is unique

You hear His call

You hear it clear

You know His voice

But you still have a choice

To follow the Shepherd

Oh, the experiences you will have

When you follow His voice

The closeness comes when you let Him lead

He will take you to your destiny

Intimacy with the Shepherd

There's no better place

And if you wander He will come after you

Because He loves you and cares for you

You hear His call

You hear it clear

You know His voice

But you still have a choice

To follow the Shepherd

He knows you can be stubborn and

Want your own way

You have a choice who to obey

You listen to other voices, and they lead you astray

For a time it may seem like the right way

Until you realize it's the voice of the enemy

The Shepherd is calling you

Pursuing you...

You know His voice

It is just for you

And it is unique

You still have a choice

Only the true Shepherd will take

You to your destiny

Intimacy with the Shepherd

23

Song of the Disciple

I remember when I was called to follow Jesus. I was only twenty.

To be a follower of Jesus Christ filled me with such excitement to begin this lifelong journey. I quickly realized that I needed to study His life in the living Word, because how could I follow someone I didn't truly know?

First, I learned what it means to be a disciple, which is "a lifelong learner of Jesus Christ," so that I could then disciple others.

The Great Commission is the calling of discipleship.

Jesus says in Matthew 28:19, "Go therefore and make disciples of all nations, baptizing them in the name of the Father and of the Son and of the Holy Spirit." So I sing the Song of the Disciple.

Oh, what a day when Jesus calls your name

Out of darkness and into the light

When Jesus calls you into a life with Him

He says,

"Follow me and I will make you fishers of men"

Oh, the faith it takes to follow His voice

He says, "My yoke is easy and My burden is light"

Our Creator God, has a grand plan to carry out

Nothing—no, nothing—can thwart

We take the next step

So we follow Jesus by faith

So we follow Jesus by faith

We learn along the way

To obey

We share the Good News of our Savior

Wherever we may go

"Baptizing in the name of the Father, the Son, and the
Holy Ghost"

Oh, what a day when Jesus calls your name out of darkness and into the light

Oh, what a day when Jesus calls your name to follow Him and be

Fishers of men

To deny yourself

Take up your cross

To be transformed

Into the image of Christ

To save your life, you lose it

For Christ

To give up the world, but gain

Your soul

All for His glory

To the One who called your name

Out of darkness into the light!

This is a lifelong journey

And then

We get to share in eternity

With the One who called your name

With the One who called your name

All for His glory

All for His glory

Oh, what a marvelous day

Oh, what a marvelous day

Song of Awareness

The song I sing today is of awareness

Awareness of my

Sin

What my flesh is capable of

Thank you LORD for your Holy Spirit in me

The battle is real

Every moment a fight. Who will win?

Although all my sins are forgiven as a believer

Because of Christ's death

Resurrection and ascension to heaven

Every moment, the battle is real

Who will win the fight in my daily life—the flesh or

The Holy Spirit?

Every moment, awareness of my sin

What my flesh is capable of

The chaos it can cause

But Christ in me

You help me overcome

Thank you, LORD, for the Holy Spirit

Christ in me

Every moment, awareness

Every moment, awareness

As I focus on you, O LORD

While I still have breath in this life

Please, LORD, let it be the Holy Spirit in me

Who wins the fight

For I am aware of what my flesh is capable of

My sin that causes chaos

But Christ in me, the One who has overcome

The battle is won when I walk

In the Holy Spirit, moment by moment

The battle is won

But Christ in me

The One who has overcome!

While I still have breath in this life

Please, LORD, let it be the Holy Spirit in me

Who wins the fight

Because every moment I am aware of what

My flesh is capable of—

But Christ in me!

My Hope and Glory!

But Christ in me!

My Hope and Glory!

I am not God...
nor do I want
to be. And so I
can rest in His
sovereignty

Song of Truth

The moment I came to understand this truth about God was when I read this passage: "For My thoughts are not your thoughts, neither are your ways My ways, declares the Lord. For as the heavens are higher than the earth, so are My ways higher than your ways and My thoughts than your thoughts." (Isaiah 55:8-9).

There are so many things in life that do not make any sense to me, but this I can believe: "That I am not God, and I won't understand. His ways are not my ways…" So I sing the Song of Truth.

God sees the beginning and the end

Everything in between

Because He is the Alpha and Omega

At times I can only see what is right in front of me

Then I am reminded of God's sovereignty

I can take a deep breath and a sigh of relief

Because the God of the Universe has total authority

The days I do look back on, my only regret is that I would have

Let go of trying to control

So today, as I face some events that make no

Sense to me

I remember what the Lord proclaims

"Your ways are not My ways…"

And then I can rest

Knowing that as the heavens are higher than my ways

And His thoughts are higher than my thoughts

This I can believe

This I can believe

I am not God

Nor do I want to be—

And so I can rest in

His sovereignty

Song of Grace

Grace

I did not earn it

I did not deserve it

A wretch like me

Your saving grace, O Lord

It consumes me

It overwhelms me

It never ends

You chose me

You, O Lord, called me out of darkness

And into the light of Your saving grace

I did not earn it

I did not deserve it

A wretch like me

You, O Lord, could see

My pain and agony

And never let me go

Your amazing grace

It consumes me

It overwhelms me

It never ends

It is hard to understand

But I believe

But I believe

Oh, I believe

You, O Lord, hear my cry in prayer

When the desperation sets in

When I am at my end

You answer in Your way and time

By Your loving grace

You, O Lord, hold me in the palm of Your hand

When all around is falling down

When the enemy is haunting

You send Your angel armies to protect those

I am praying for

Those I love

It is all too hard to understand

But I trust

YOUR

Ways

YOUR

Amazing grace

It consumes me

It overwhelms me

It never ends

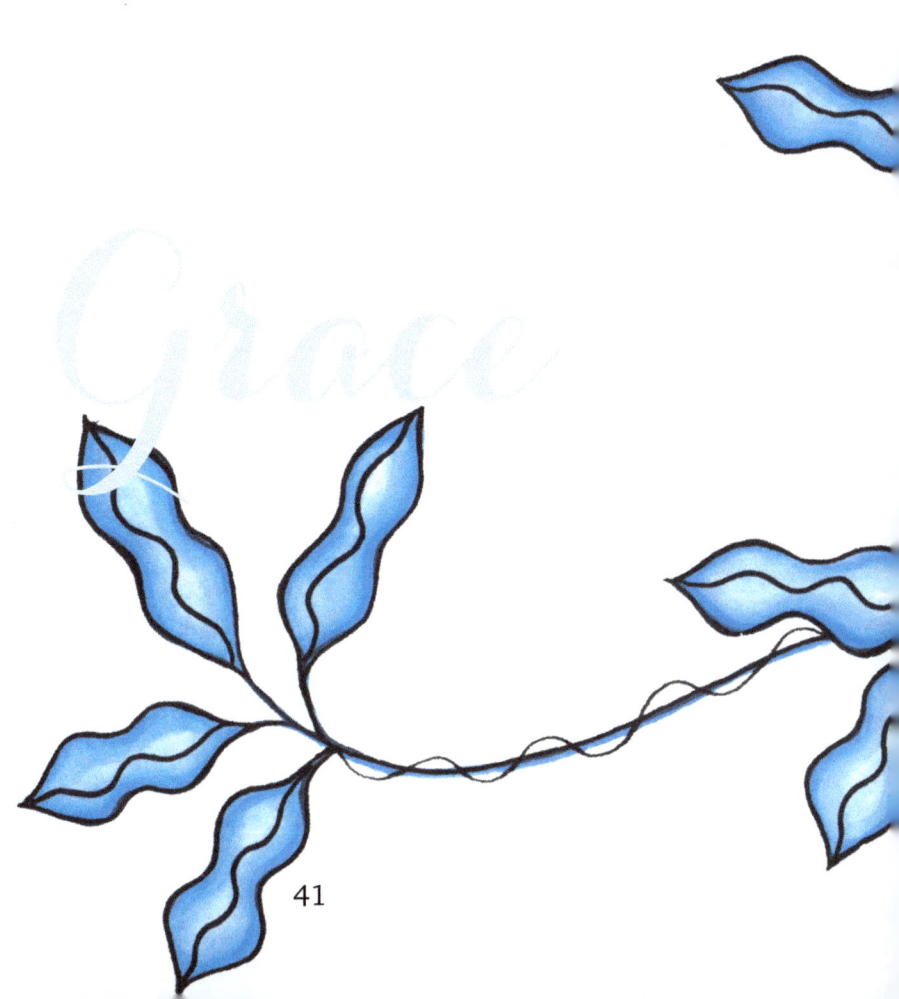

41

Come to the Cross of Christ and be cleansed with God's truth

Song of Repentance

I come to the cross of Christ

And confess

It's where I find rest

I turn from my sins

To the Lord

My Master

Savior

I adore

I come to the cross of Christ

It's where my burdens go

To rest

Turn, turn, turn

From sin

To the Lord

Master

Savior

I adore

Come to the cross of Christ and lay down

Your addictions,

Afflictions, and abuse,

And be cleansed with God's truth

Come to the cross of Christ and confess

Discover your purpose

Turn, turn, turn

From all your past sin

to the Lord

Master

Savior

You adore

It's where your suffering begins to make sense

Turn, turn, turn

To the Lord

Master

Savior

You now adore—

It's a love you've never had before

Come to the cross of Christ and give thanks

For the victory

Now you have a story

A song to sing of repentance

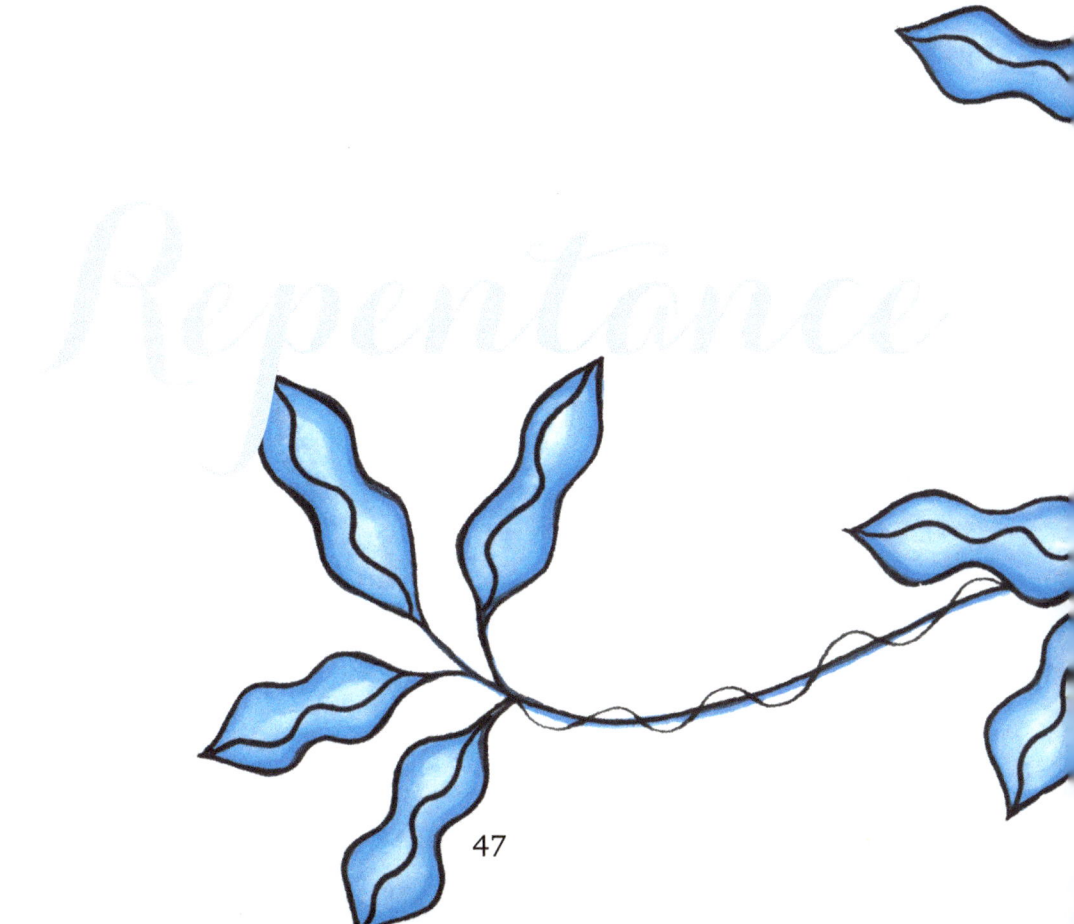

47

Song of New Creation

My name is New Creation

The old is gone

It has been wiped away

Like the new day dawn

My sin is forgiven

And my past is cast into the sea of

Forgetfulness

My name is New Creation

It is given by the Savior, Christ

It is only because of what He did on Calvary

Jesus took sin upon Himself and died

Jesus rose from the dead on the third day

And lives forever

Jesus conquered death!

My name is New Creation

In Christ

Christ in me

Christ in me

Christ in me

My name is New Creation

The old is gone

The new has come

Inspired by

2 Corinthians 5:17

Song of the Poem

I learned recently that the Greek word for workmanship is *Poemia*. Ephesians 2:10 tells us that, "We are His workmanship, created in Christ Jesus for good works, which God prepared beforehand, that we should walk in them." We are God's poem, His work of art … a masterpiece. So I sing the Song of the Poem.

Lord, you say we are a poem

Created by Your hands

For Your pleasure

You say we are a work of art

A masterpiece, unique

For You to enjoy

Forever

You say we are Your workmanship

Created in Christ Jesus for good works

Lord, You say You prepared them before the foundation

Of the earth

You say we should walk in them

We are

Your masterpiece

Your poem

Your workmanship

You say we are valuable

A poem created by Your divine hand

For Your pleasure forever

You, O Lord

Love without measure

A Father forever

Your grace is a treasure

Please, help me Lord, to walk in the good works

You have prepared for me alone

You say I am your poem

Tell the "Voice of Image," "I am a child of the King"

Song of Image

Reflecting on the verse, "Be still, and know that I am God," stopped me in my tracks one day and that became the moment I realized all my activity and my busyness was just a cover for my wrong motives, as if I could hide in my performance and service for God. It was a show, but wasn't everything?

Image, oh image, what everyone thinks, sees, and knows about me.

This behavior was learned early in my childhood, before I had a relationship with Jesus, but I carried this same trap into my relationship with Him as an adult. So I sing the Song of Image.

Oh Image, Oh Image

Let me

Silence you

Image…

You taught me to stay busy

Hide the truth

When I was young

Image screamed

"Good girl

Good job

Be pretty

Look at me

But

Hide the truth

put it all away"

Image now screams

"Be a good Christian

Be a good wife

Handle everyone's strife

Be pretty, be kind

What do people think?

Don't show the real you!"

Until one day a voice breaks through

"Let ME silence you

Let ME silence you

Be still, and know that I am God"

Image is silenced

HIS voice says it all

Be still

Let ME

Tell you who you are!

You are more than a conqueror

You are a Child of the King

You are beautifully and wonderfully made

You are a masterpiece

You are no longer a slave to your compulsions

You are My temple

You are My friend

You are held in the palm of My hand

"Be still, and know that I am God"

Now when

The voice of Image creeps in…

I

Tell the voice of Image

I am a Child of the King!

Image,

I am no longer your friend.

Image is silenced

Image is silenced

"Be still, and know that I am God."
—*Psalm 46:10*

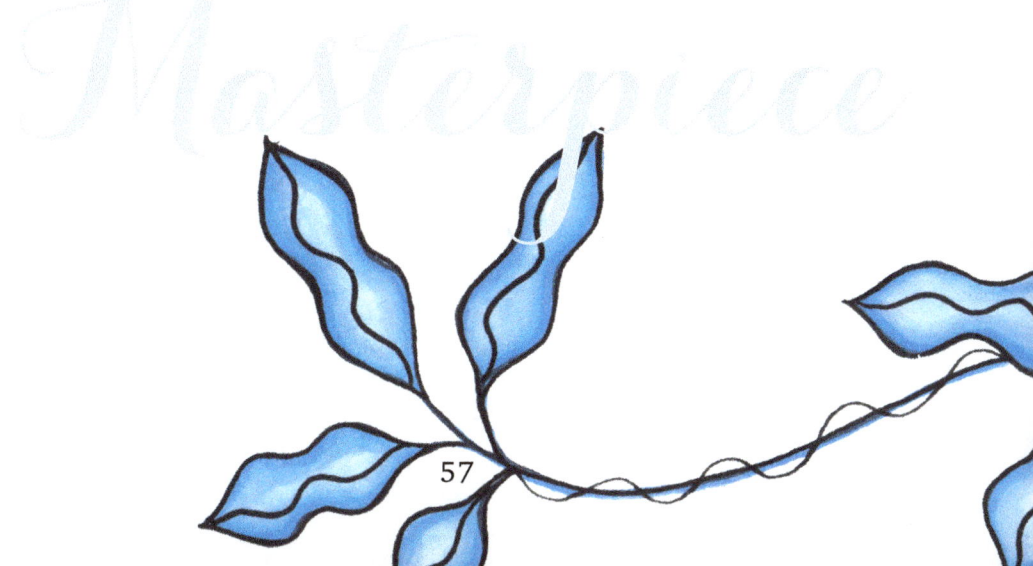

57

Song of the Enemy

Oh, he has a song.

It's the song that comes when you are worn out, burnt out, and spent

Life, oh life

If you are old enough, you can remember albums

The needle would get stuck on part of the song

It would repeat over and over until you move the needle

The album was probably scratched—

Like the enemy's voice, stuck on repeat

The song he sings in your mind...

"You're no good, you're no good, you're no good"

Or, "You are a failure, failure, failure

You are ugly, ugly, ugly"

Playing on repeat

Make it stop

Like the needle playing on that album on repeat

Because it is scratched, worn out…

It's been played too long

Those songs the enemy plays to thwart

God's plan for your life

Put on a new song

Listen to the voice of God singing over you

His Word says you are a Child of the Most High God

You are More Than a Conqueror through Christ our Lord

You have the mind of Christ

You are a child of light

You have freedom in Christ

You have a calling on your life

The enemy's song will sneak in…

Learn to know which voice is singing over you

Song of Miracles

The moment I realized I needed a miracle, I was twenty years old. I had become a slave to my three-year battle with bulimia, an eating disorder that had me in chains.

Who could free me?

I am so afflicted

Darkness surrounds me

My mind races

What could ease this pain?

Who could set me free?

Memories of my past flash and haunt my mind as if they are real

I want to numb the thoughts…

How do I go on?

I have tried everything I know

Trying, trying, trying…

It only eases the pain, but for a moment

Now it's back stronger

Guilt and Shame become my best friends as we hide in the darkness together

I try to purge my past

Release it out of my body

This becomes my life

I don't want to feel

My feelings hurt others

I no longer have a voice

Walls closing in

Alone and afraid

Does anyone else feel like me?

Am I the only one?

I cry out to God in the dark

Please help me!

In the silence, a voice breaks through—

This voice was different, it was calming

I listen to the whisper in the dark

"Open the Bible and read the book of John"

I obey

I read, read, read

I knew of God, and as I read the Bible, could it be true?

That Jesus is God? John 10:30

That Jesus came to save the lost like me?

I related to the woman at the well, who was so full of shame
that she came alone

A man at the pool waiting so long for his healing, and his time
had finally come

Could Jesus today heal my affliction?

Could Jesus redeem me from all my sins?

Give me eternal life with God?

In the silence, I am led to pray, pray, pray—

"God, if You are real, please heal me like the woman at the well

I promise to shout Your name, Jesus, in the streets

I will follow You and serve You the rest of my life

I believe You can heal me"

The Lord, in His grace, chose to rescue and redeem me that night out of the dark pit, out of my

Addiction and sin

The next morning comes—

I emerge out of darkness and into the day!

The compulsion to eat and purge was gone!

That emptiness was gone

I was now a new creation in Christ

The old was gone

That was over forty years ago and I am still reading my Bible and listening to God speak to me

I sing His praises in the day

I sing of the lessons I have learned in the dark, as God teaches me in the valley, the storm, the fire, but also in the joy of following Jesus Christ

Like the songbird, who hears his father's voice in the dark, and emerges in the day with a beautiful song to sing—

I am the Songbird!

You, my friend, are the Songbird!

Now I want to hear your song—

What has God taught you in the dark?

Will you join me in this great singing adventure?

This is the song I sing today—

The Song of Miracles

What did I learn that dark night?

Jesus is the miracle I was searching for

Yes, I was delivered from my eating disorder, but the real miracle was my Savior, Jesus Christ, redeeming me from my sins

Giving me what I really longed for—

A relationship with God, my Creator, forever

A purpose to serve Him forever

The miracle is we are never alone in the dark

Song of Victory

Remember who I am…

My child

When you are following

My plan

Don't be alarmed by the attacks of the enemy at hand

For Satan spends his time

Trying to throw you off track

It's in these moments

Remember who I am

And who you are

My child

Remember My Word to keep

You strong

Remember that I have the victory in

The end

Remember that you are filled with

The Spirit

So our battle is won

But for now you are on

The front line

But you are not alone

The battle is real

Remember My Word

To keep you stronger

Remember the battle is not against

Flesh and blood

Those you love

Remember who I am

The victory

Is won!

Inspired by

Ephesians 6:12

71

Song of Serendipity

This song came about one day when I was feeling sad because all my plans had fallen apart. So I found myself left alone. Then I began to listen to the wrong voice in my head. Ever have days like these? Going down a negative path? I certainly do. What do you do? I prayed … then I felt led to go sit outdoors by myself.

Little did I know that I would meet a sweet soul—not planned by me…but by Serendipity.

So this is the song I wrote that day, The Song of Serendipity.

Make room for the Holy Spirit

Make margin in your day for the unexpected delight—

The serendipity of life

Make space for conversations to take place

Not everything needs to be planned

Make moments for new memories to unfold

Make time to listen to the still, small voice

Make your encounters have meaning

The serendipity of life

Make room for the Holy Spirit to move

In and through you

Make choices to align with God's Word

And watch what He does—

Serendipity

Little did I know that I would meet a sweet soul

When all my plans fell apart that day

My sadness turned into

An unexpected delight

When I listen to that still, small voice

Make room...

Serendipity

Song of All-Knowing

Oh child, I am calling you to Myself today

Simply nothing else

To do

But be with Me

I know your life has not turned out how you thought it might be

Please trust Me I AM working it all out

According to MY plans and purpose for you

I can take the disappointment and the evil that you have endured

And turn it to good—please be assured

For I know you love Me

I know you have sins you still struggle with and you come to
Me daily and confess

I know your struggle is with your flesh—

The world you are living in

When I look at you, I see someone who repents

Please remember, dear child of Mine

You can call on the Holy Spirit any time—

We have not left you alone

Oh child, I am calling you to Myself

Simply nothing else to do

But be with Me, Your Father

And know I have you covered

And know I have you covered

I know what you have overcome

I know what you are working on

Remember you are not alone

I know it's hard to comprehend how I enjoy your presence

So child, I am calling you to Myself today

I know you share in My burden for the lost

I hear your prayers

I know your joy comes from seeing others discover Me and

Seeing them overcome

Oh child, I am calling you to Myself today

Simply nothing else

And you will discover

I have you covered

I have you covered

I have you covered

Song of Fire

My own experience with fire has taught me that it can bring warmth to a very cold night. Fire can also be dangerous when out of control. It can burn and explode, bringing about death and destruction. Fire can also refine and purify, making something beautiful in its time.

God is described in the Bible as a consuming fire (Deuteronomy 4:24; Hebrews 12:29; Isaiah 64:8).

I have experienced all of the fires above. Have you? Have you experienced the consuming fire of God in your life?

There is purpose in God's fire.

The consuming fire of God gives us our own story to tell.

So I sing the Song of Fire.

Until you have been through God's all-consuming fire

Until the Potter has His time at the wheel

Molding

Shaping

Spinning

Creating His vision for you

His hand perfecting at the Potter's wheel

Until His kiln has done its work

Let it burn

Let the fire consume

Let it purify

You won't be in the fire one minute too long

You are not alone

You are with your Master Creator

Until you have been through the refining fire meant just for you

And the Potter says He's done

Let it burn

Let the fire consume

Let it purify

Not one minute too long

You are not alone

And when you emerge from your fire

Meant just for you

You will have a story to tell

Because everything is made beautiful in

God's time

For the Potter's purpose

For the Potter's glory

Now you have a story to tell

The story of your time at the Potter's wheel

And in the fire

You were not alone

The Master Creator always finishes what He started

Making you beautiful in His time

Your Song of Fire!

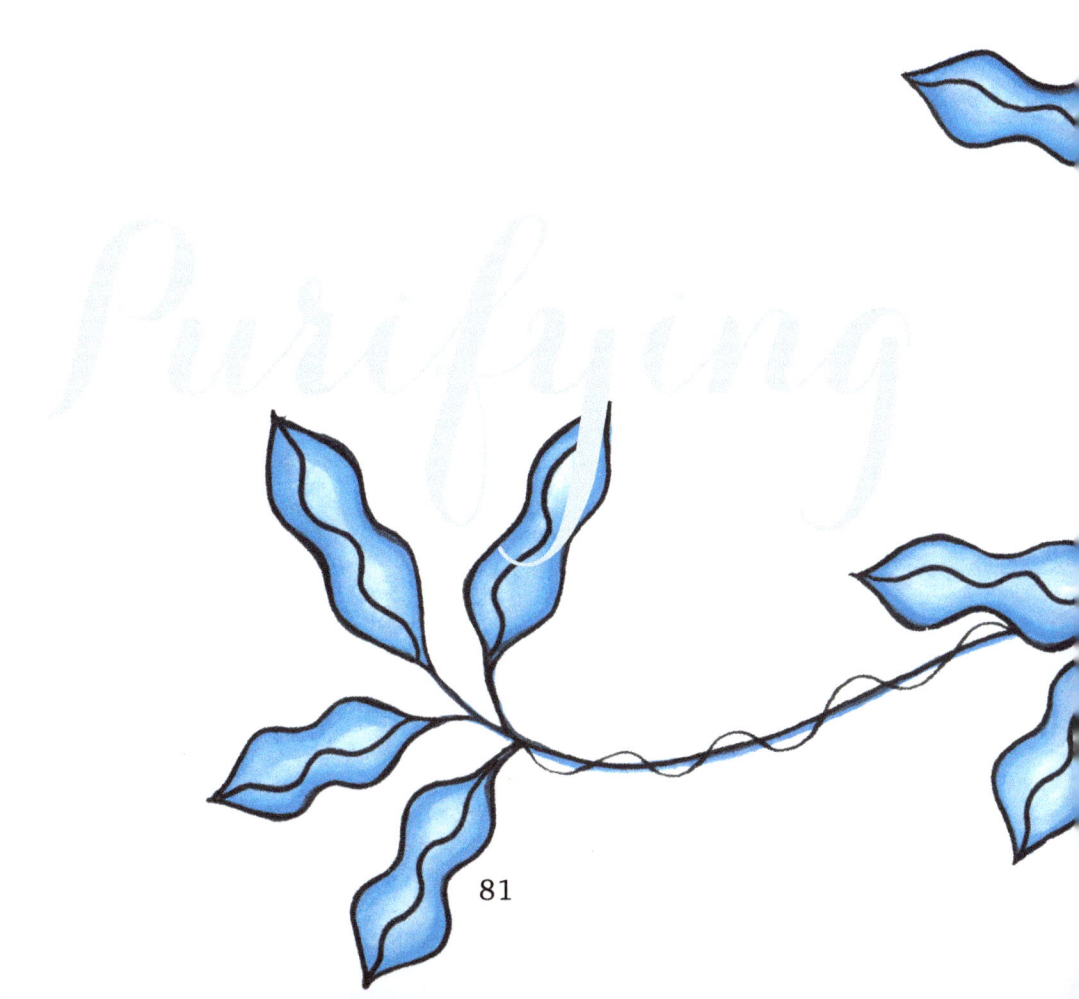

81

Song of Solitude

For three years, I filled my time alone with an eating disorder, bulimia. I know now that it was an attempt to control something in my life. I had a lot of childhood trauma that was never dealt with, and I numbed the pain with this addiction. Who wants to feel something they don't understand? The day I was set free from this addiction of bulimia by the saving grace of Jesus Christ, I was able to replace this time alone with reading my Bible. I am grateful God led me to a healthy relationship with Him. I was anxious at times in just *being,* but as years passed I became more and more comfortable being alone, because I knew God was with me.

Solitude became my friend. It's different from loneliness. Now I can just sit in nature with no agenda. I remember before Solitude was my friend, I would be in a room full of people and still feel alone.

Now I can hear the birdsongs or the rustling of the wind in the trees and enjoy the beauty all around me.

I can enjoy God and worship the Creator who made all of creation. So I sing the Song of Solitude.

In Solitude

I am rid of the noise

In Solitude, I can hear God's voice

In Solitude, I began to feel

And therefore heal

In Solitude, I can be real

In Solitude, I can process my pain

In Solitude, there is so much to gain

In Solitude, I am never alone

Solitude is my friend

In Solitude, is where I begin to find meaning

It's where I can hear God's voice

Singing over me

It's the Song of Solitude

For God sings

I am always with you

I will never leave you

Nor forsake you

Singing over me

Song of Seeking

Lord, help me to seek Thee

When my day seems long

Or my day seems short

Help me to seek Thee

In victory or strain

Always seeking You for guidance in

The joy and pain

Help me be led by Your Spirit in me

Help me to seek Thy wisdom for all

My steps

I don't want to take one without You

For I easily stumble in my sin when

I am not guided by You

Help me, Lord, the steadfast One

To seek Thee when my day seems short

Or my day seems long

Help me turn to You in humility

For I am aware of my fragility in my

Pride

Please help me seek Thee before I fall

Into temptation from the world

Help me, Lord, my Protector

From the evil one

When my day seems long

Or my day is short

I seek Thee

It's in the valley where you learn the most

Song of the Valley

Come down from the mountaintop where you learn to boast

It's in the valley that you learn the most

It's in the valley where you hear My voice

In the silence, I meet you in your lowest point

When you are humble and contrite

Come down from the mountaintop where you learn to boast

It's in your sorrow where you experience My grace the most

Come away from your doing and distractions, and meet Me in
the stillness

Come down from the mountaintop where you learn to boast

It's in your pain where you learn to listen to Me the most

You won't know Me until you share in My suffering

So put away your striving, and meet Me in the quiet

Come down from the mountaintop where you look for man's approval and applause

In My Word, you will find what you are looking for…

Is Me—

Your LORD who loves you the most.

Come down

Come down

Come down

And you will discover

There is so much more

Than you can see

A life waiting

A life with Me in Eternity

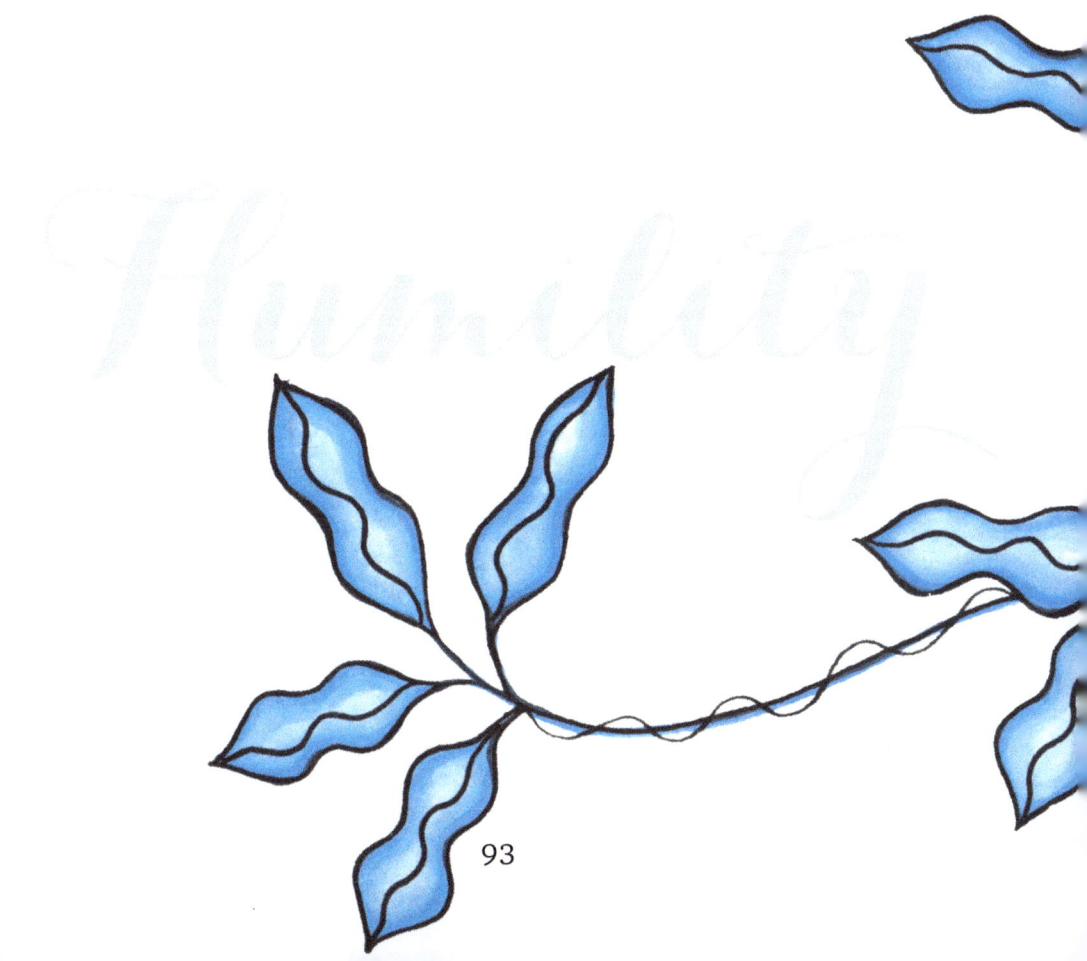

93

Song of Lingering

I hear the voice of God

Telling me to go…

And yet I linger

But God understands my hesitation

So, He takes my hand as we step

Into the unknown

Known to God

Unknown to me

For God is with me

So I'm not afraid to go

I hear the voice of God

Telling me to go—

Take the next step

This time I don't hesitate

As He takes my hand

Into the unknown

Known to God

Unknown to me

No longer afraid

For God is with me

Every step of the way

Learning to trust

Instead of linger—

I hear the voice of God

Telling me, "No

Don't go

Into the unknown"

This time I want to go

Full force

The Lord takes my hand

And holds me back

For God knows when I should go

And when I should stay

So my job is to obey …

The voice of God

Trusting

Now I am free to sing the song You have given me

Song of His Way

Have you ever noticed in your life that simple phrases can have a huge impact on your thinking? Many years ago when I was learning God's Word, one of my Bible teachers posed the question, "What if you allowed God to have HIS way in your life? What could happen?" I soon realized in order to let God have HIS way, I needed to know His ways. So this meant for me more praying, more studying His Word, and more asking for guidance. I came to find out that early Christ followers were called "The Way." Jesus said, "I am the way, and the truth, and the life. No one comes to the Father except through me" (John 14:6). I appreciate pastors and Bible teachers for their diligent study of Scripture and their gift to bring application to an audience. I have always liked challenges … so now I challenge you! What if Jesus were to have His way in your life? So I sing the Song of HIS Way.

What can I say as I let you go into the world

To make your way…

So many choices to make

Along the way

It's up to you—

The path you take to the right

Or to the left

But please know there is the best way

The narrow path

that you can choose

It's up to you

It's MY WAY

The narrow gate

That you enter and it leads to ME

To the truth and to the life…

To intimacy

What can I say as I let you go

Into the world

To make your way…

I hope you will choose the best way

Call on My name

It leads you to the truth, life, and intimacy

Once you choose this narrow path

You will not want to go back

Although the temptations of this

World and its traps

Beckon and call, and proclaim

You are missing out—

But in your resolve you will shout!

Please will you join Me and take the narrow path

That leads to truth and to life

And to

Eternity

You are not missing out!

If the narrow path is what you have been

Searching for—

I hope you will choose My WAY

I am the WAY, the Truth, and the Life

No one comes to the Father, except through Me

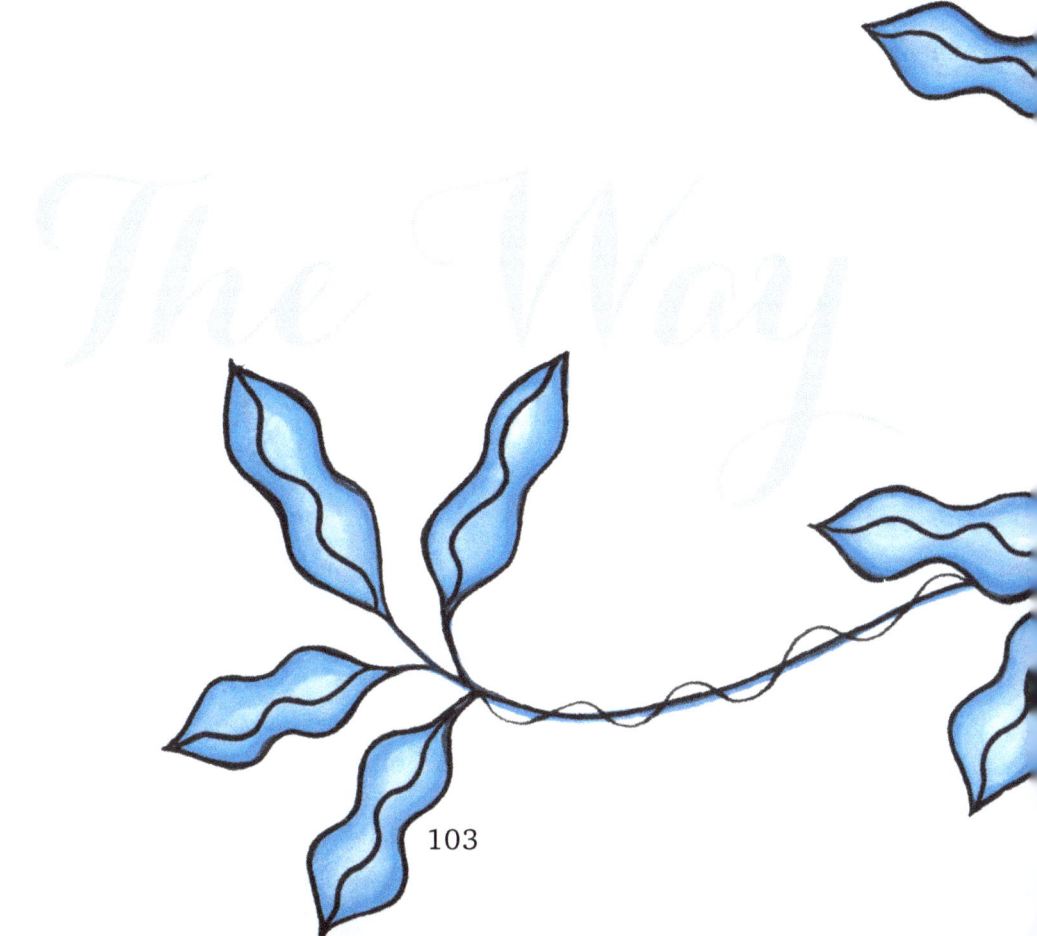

Song of Sitting

When there are no words for a friend who was just diagnosed with cancer. Or perhaps a loved one has just lost a friend. Or someone shares news that is too devastating to bear...

Have you ever been there?

Nothing to say.

But I pray.

I sing the Song of Sitting.

Sitting quietly with my friend

Nothing to say, but silence cuts the air

It feels so uncomfortable

And then You, O Lord enter in

You are quiet

Your presence, Lord, is enough

Your comfort fills the air—

Then saying nothing

Becomes everything

Because we are not alone

Sitting quietly with my friend

Will never be the same

Because You, O Lord, have entered in

Your presence is enough

Your presence is enough

Your presence is enough

Your comfort fills the air

Sitting quietly with my friend

Will never be the same

I have no words to say

But Your presence

Says everything

Song of God's Timing

Today I sing the Song of God's Timing!

God's timing is perfect in every way

I pray

I pray

I pray

For God's will and His way!

I admit I don't always understand

Although I trust His hand

This is where my hope comes rushing in

Like the wind

For God's timing is perfect in every way

So I pray

I pray

I pray

As I wait upon You, Lord

This is where my patience comes rushing in—

I admit I don't always understand

So today I sing the Song of God's Timing

It's never too early

Never too late

His timing is perfect in every way

God's will and His way

I admit I don't always understand

But I trust His hand

Over time and experience

I can now say

God's timing is perfect in every way

So I wait upon You, Lord

And pray

Pray

Pray

This is where my faith comes rushing in—

Like the wind

I learn to trust

Your voice over and over again—

The promises You keep from Your Word

Today I sing the Song of God's Timing

And I pray and I wait...

God is perfect in every way!

God is perfect in every way!

Promises

109

Song of Inspiration

Sometimes divine inspiration

comes from our desperation—

When we run out of our own devices and

Nothing we do or say is sufficing

In our state of desperation and

When our own calculations

Come to an end—

The divine can begin

Sometimes divine inspiration comes

When all is said and done

And nothing in life makes sense to us

When trying in our own strength to

Figure it out

Divine inspiration comes at a time

We let go

Divine inspiration comes when we let

God take control

God, Your will, not mine

When we realize

Creator God Almighty

Has been in charge this whole time—

Oh, Divine Inspiration

Oh, Divine Inspiration

Your way, not mine

Your way, not mine

Song of My Pen

I can get lost in my writing

It is when my thoughts

Melt my pen

The ink begins to flow

The thoughts once trapped in my mind

Come out

They are alive

The words written on the page

Now bring meaning to the

Joys and sorrows of life

God meets me there between my

Thoughts and pen

I begin to see life differently

All the time I have spent with God in

Solitude…

Is now a song

On my pen

Waiting to be written

Waiting to be written

No longer trapped—

When God meets me there

Between my thoughts and my pen

I get lost in our time together

Thoughts melt my pen

The ink begins to flow

I have a new song to sing

I have a new song to sing

Waiting to be written

Waiting to be written

No longer trapped

Song of Breakthrough

I am not sure what kind of breakthrough you are praying for. This Song of Breakthrough was one that came very unexpectedly.

It is now one of my favorites.

I hope you see why.

It was a whisper one day when I was so admittedly frustrated over all the circumstances in my life. I was crying out to God, basically in surrender. I was out of answers. So I sing the Song of Breakthrough.

Awaiting

Anticipating

For a breakthrough

For God to heal all the hurt

Praying

Awaiting

To break through

That addiction that has overcome

The one we love

Praying

Awaiting

Watching the world turn dark

Right before my eyes

Breakthrough

Won't you please come?

Praying

Awaiting

For that one relationship to heal

For the grief to go away

For fear of what may come

Praying

Awaiting

For a breakthrough

And then You break through

O LORD

You are the Breakthrough

I have been praying for

You are the Breakthrough

You are the discovery

I have been awaiting

O LORD

YOU are the Breakthrough

I have been praying for

You are the Song of Breakthrough

You have been listening to my cries

Hearing my frustration

Waiting … anticipating for me to see

You, Jesus, are the only Breakthrough that I need

You alone, Lord, are the Blessing, the Favor, and

My Answered Prayer!

Every breakthrough I have desired is found in YOU!

YOU are the Breakthrough I have been longing for

Nothing has changed in my circumstance,

But

How

I

See

YOU!

I now see YOU as my Breakthrough!

Jesus, thank YOU

Jesus, thank YOU

YOU alone are the Blessing, the Favor

The Answer To Prayer!

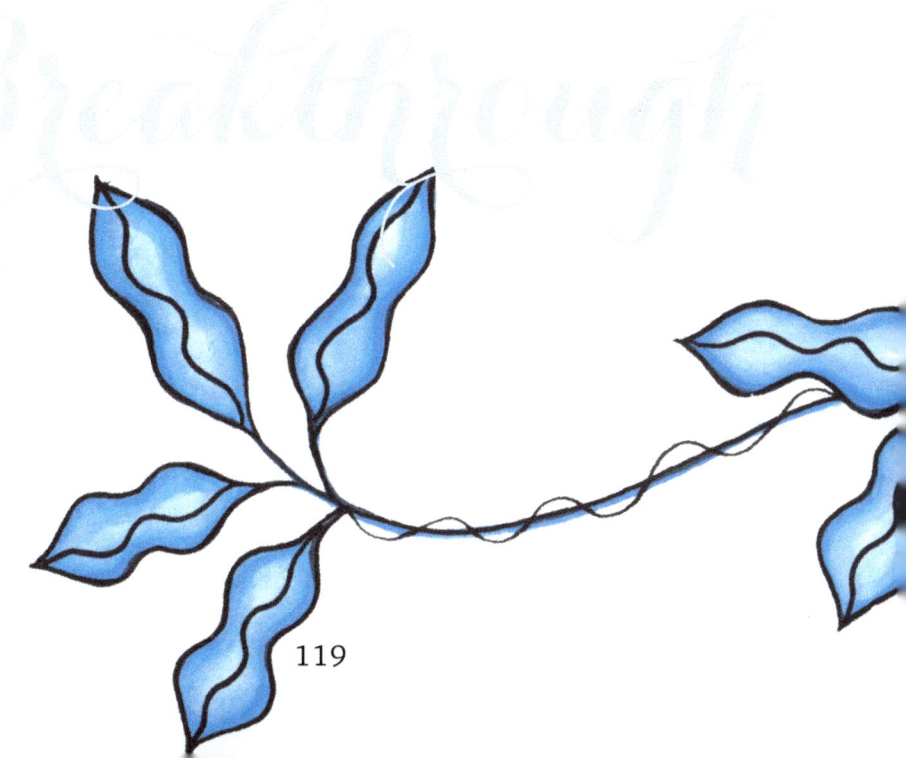

Song of Gratitude

Anxiety creeps in

I can hear my heart beating rapidly

I take a deep breath, hold it

Exhale

I think thoughts of You, Lord

Gratitude comes in

And comforts like a friend

Reminding me of where I have been

And whose I am...

I spend time with my Savior, Jesus

Listening

Soaking in His presence

Gratitude steps in

Attitude changes

I spend time with Gratitude

I do this several times a day

When anxiety creeps in—

I take a deep breath

And thank Him

Gratitude

Reminds me of whose I am

Soaking in His presence

All my fears disappear

I do this several times a day

Gratitude

Enters in—

Gratitude

You change everything!

Join me

Take a deep breath

Hold it

Exhale

Think thoughts of Jesus

Gratitude

You change everything!

123

II

Emerging Out of Darkness and Singing in the Light

Song of the Bright Morning Star

As God laid the foundation of the earth

Dear Bright Morning Star

From beginning, You have been

Along with the angels praising over the Creator's mighty hand

Rejoicing as the Spirit hovers over the dark waters

Rejoicing as the Father ushers in all that He had planned

Praising the King

Praising the One who laid the cornerstone

And ushered in the wind

Oh, what a joy from the beginning it must have been

It was glorious! It was glorious! It was glorious!

Dear Bright Morning Star

You were there when God called in the day and night

When God created man

What a sight it must have been

To rejoice in the heavens

Singing as the Father ushered in all that He had planned

Then God walked with man and woman in the garden

Oh, what a joy that must have been

They were asked to not eat of one tree

Otherwise they were free

They had a choice

Then in came sin

When the deceiver stepped in

They chose to eat of the forbidden tree

And it changed everything

Their rebellion separated man from a Holy God

Now they knew of death

But God ushered in His plan of redemption

Dear Bright Morning Star, from beginning You have been

You are the Plan!

You are the Plan!

The Plan Of Redemption!

You humbled Yourself and came to earth to serve us all

The only God Man to suffer death on a cross for man's sin

To be resurrected

And ascended

It is glorious! It is glorious! It is glorious!

To be lifted high

Dear Bright Morning Star

Now we can be reconciled to Holy God

Now You pursue us

As we call upon Your name, Jesus!

Oh, what a day!

The Name that saves us from darkness into light

The Name that has healing in His wings

The Name who gives hope for a new day

And now we behold His sovereignty

It is glorious! It is glorious! It is glorious!

As all that He had planned unfolds

Together we praise our King

Together we praise our King

And one day the Bright Morning Star

Who is lifted high

Will welcome us into eternity

Those who have overcome

Those who are written in the Lamb's book of life

Oh, what a joy

Oh, what a joy

Oh, what a joy

Dear Bright Morning Star

Lifted high

We sing praises to You, Our King!

We sing praises to You, Our King!

Forever!

You were the Plan from the beginning!

Inspired by

Revelation 22:16, Numbers 24:17

Song of New Life

This song came about as a result of my many years leading a Bible study at the Changing Lives Center in Phoenix, Arizona. Many women and children have come through this life-changing program. I count it a privilege to get to see transformed lives because of Jesus Christ. This song is inspired by the countless women who have changed my life through watching Jesus change theirs.

"Therefore, if anyone is in Christ, he is a new creation. The old has passed away; behold, the new has come" (2 Corinthians 5:17). And so I sing the Song of New Life.

My favorite thing in life is to

Witness Jesus Christ transform a life—

Right before my very eyes

Weekly, I get to anticipate who's next

I watch it unfold

A mystery to behold

The old life crucified with Christ

The old life is gone, the new is here!

A mystery to behold

How the Holy Spirit moves

How the Holy Spirit transforms

What I can do is inspire them to look to You—

To deny themselves

To follow You, Jesus

On the path that You have already laid out

I love to witness a transformed life in Jesus Christ

I get to watch what was meant for evil

Turn to good

For Your glory

And for their good to those who love YOU

People from all walks of life

I have seen it all

When Jesus transforms a life right before my very eyes

I can't deny the power that He has

He has changed me!

It is truly my favorite thing in my life

To anticipate a changed life

As I point them to Christ...

The One who can take what was meant for evil

And turn it to your good

For His glory

and His purpose

For if anyone is in Christ Jesus,

The old life is gone, the new is here!

What a privilege and a joy!

What a privilege and a joy!

What I can do is

Inspire them to listen to You

to serve You

Then I get to watch

Their new life unfold

As they listen to You

As they serve You

Right before my very eyes!

It is my favorite thing in life!

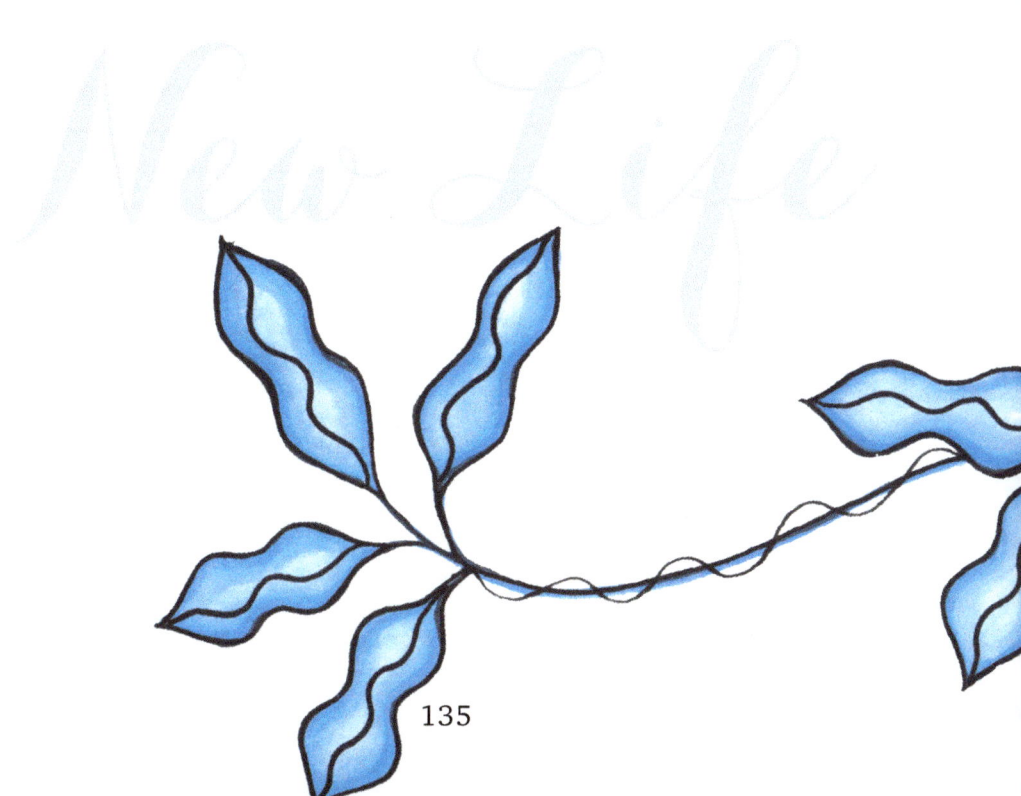

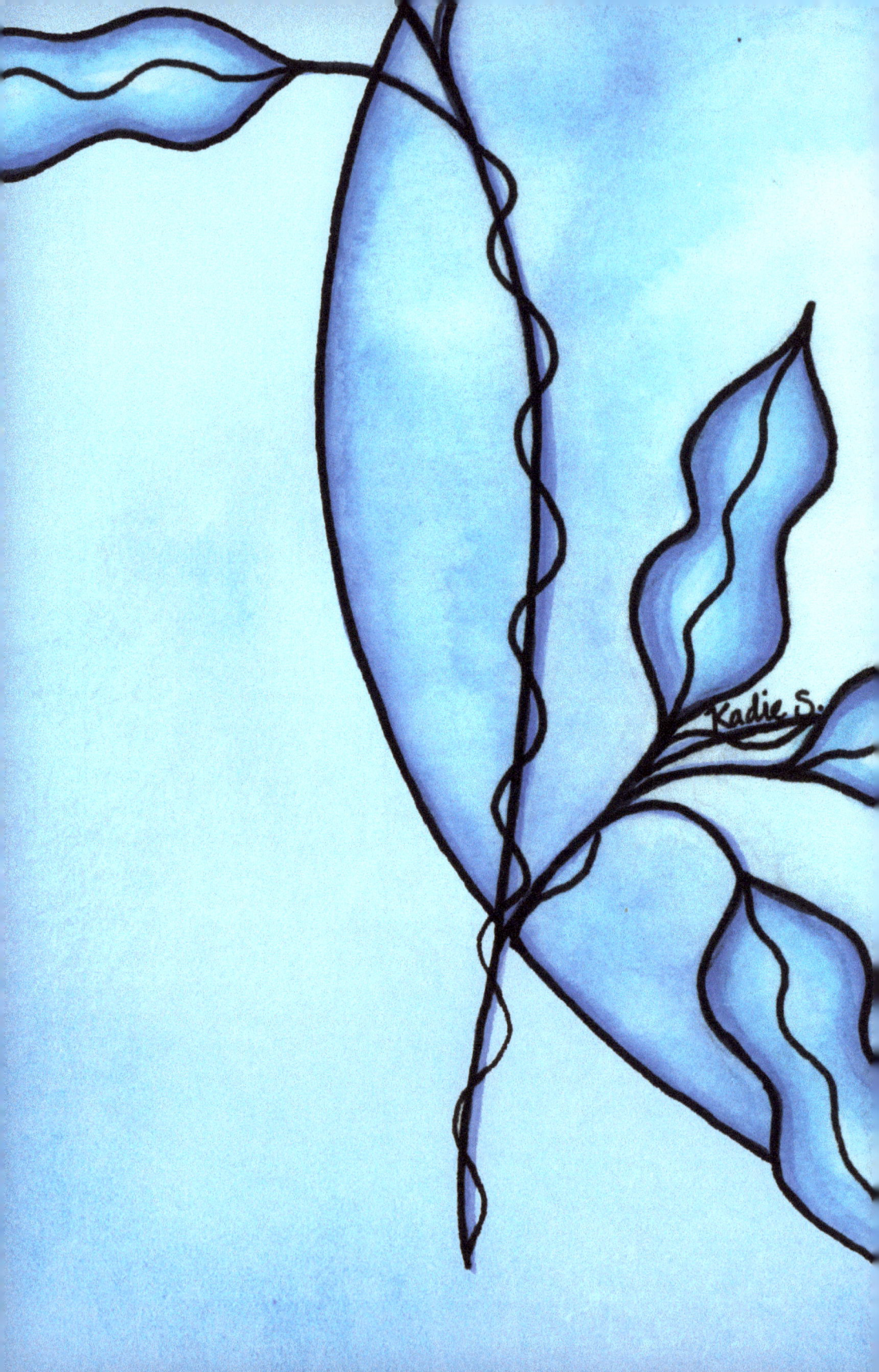

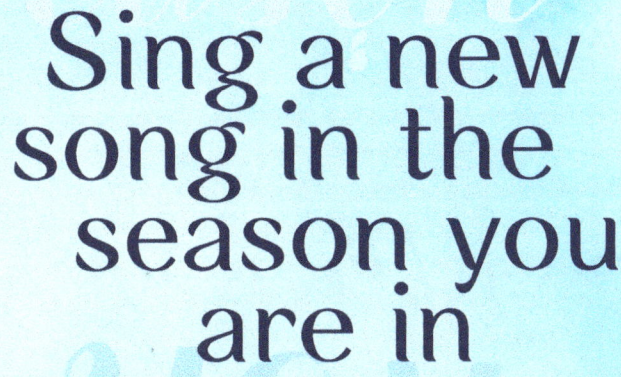

Sing a new song in the season you are in

Song of the Seasons

Let's sing a new song in the

Season we are in

For we know the season will change—

It's just a matter of time

So while you're waiting, anticipating, or just

Hoping for some change

Learn to sing a new song

To the Lord

Give Him the praise

Give Him the praise

He deserves

For we know time brings new seasons

So let's sing together the new song

In the season we are in

Enjoy the Lord while you are waiting,

Anticipating, or just hoping for some change

Give Him the praise

Give Him the praise

Give Him the praise

He deserves

Let's sing a new song

In the season we are in

Let's sing a new song

In the season we are in

Song of the Ocean

Ocean breeze settles over me

It touches in places no one has ever known

It is the Holy Spirit dancing on the breeze

Over the glistening water

I feel it on my face

And I hear You calling for me to soak

In Your presence

To feel the ocean breeze

Touch me

These times are only for You and me Lord

Ocean breeze—it touches me,

The cool mist on my face

The sand beneath my feet

The waves roll in

I am filled with gratitude

In Your presence

Tears of joy begin to flow

These times are only for You and me, Lord

As the ocean breeze touches me

As the Holy Spirit dances on the breeze

I soak in Your presence

I soak in Your presence

I soak in Your presence

Song of Friendship

I remember the day I asked God to bring like-minded friends into my life, but I also asked Him to help me be a better friend. He answered my prayer in many ways. I soon realized the purpose for friendships in my life. Some friends have been in my life for a lifetime, a season, and God has HIS reasons. Perhaps we need to travel this journey together and the friendship grows us both? So I sing the Song of Friendship.

Friendship is like a song—

We sing it together and it carries us along

We sing on the path that God has us on

Together

So much to do

See

And be

So many memories to make!

The tears

Joy

And heartache

Laughter and cheer

Some friendships stay together for a season

I believe there is a special reason

We sing together on the path God has us on

And when God says it is time to move on—

The music carries us along

To where we both belong

For the new season

God has us on

Perhaps we will pick up where we left off

When our paths cross again—

For God has a plan

Friendship is like a song

We sing on the path God has us on

My favorite thing to sing with my friends

Is praises of my Savior, Jesus

And what HE has done!

Some friendships come, we grow

And then go—

The song in the wind carries us away

To sing the Song of Friendship

With those who God puts on our path

New hopes, new memories to make

New joys, and new growth

God has a reason for this new season

As He directs our steps

One day, my hope is that we will

All sing together

In Eternity

Praises to our KING

One day, we will all sing together

Praises to our KING!

The Song of Friendship

In the new season we are in

Inspired by

Ecclesiastes 4:9-12

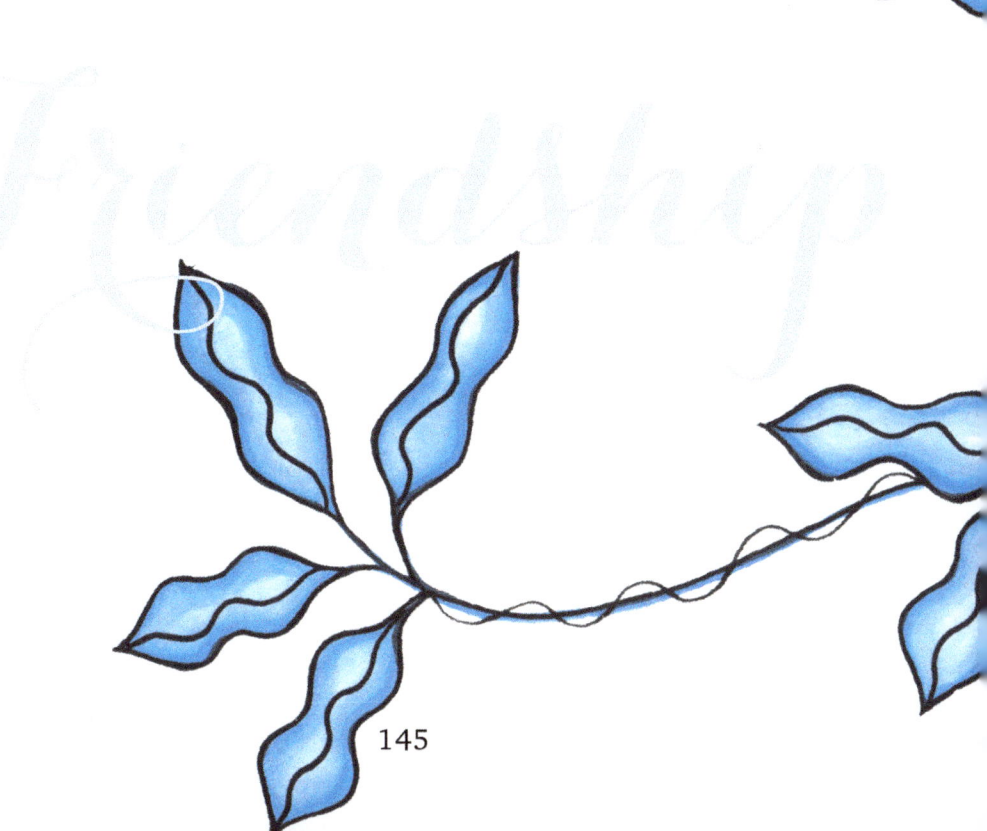

Song of My Mentor

Father, oh how You provide

So unexpectedly

A mentor chosen perfectly for me—

A spiritual guide

An encouraging voice

Who brings profound meaning to my life

She challenges me to live my life

Consecrated unto You

Whatever You call me to do

She tells me I have a voice

Something to say that You have taught me

Oh, Father, how You provide

I am so filled with gratitude

I want everything I say and do

To be consecrated unto You

To bring glory and honor to You

Alone

Thank you, Father, for providing my

Mentor

Chosen perfectly for me

A spiritual guide

An encouraging voice

Who brings profound meaning to my life

Because her life is consecrated unto You

She is beautiful

Her life reflects You

My mentor

And so we sing together

We want to bring You honor

Now and forever!

Song of the Encourager

Have you ever thought, "When I grow up I want to be more like her? Or him?" I certainly have.

When you leave a conversation with that one person and you are so encouraged in the Lord—it causes you to want to know God more… to dig into His Word more… to become more and more like Jesus…

What I mean is that there is a level of safety—because what they communicate is God's sovereignty… because they have lived enough life and walked with God through enough trials that they know God in a more intimate way. They understand how to walk in the Holy Spirit. They know God is in control. That the God of the Universe owns it all. They know they are not perfect, but are becoming more and more like Jesus. They know God is the Author and Perfector of Their Faith. This inspires me…

This encourages me.

I hope you have someone in your life like this ... I sure do!

So I sing the Song of the Encourager.

Thank you, Lord, for the encourager

The one who can see life through Your perspective

They have a way of putting away judgement

They wear the hat of mercy

They can cheer you up with just a word

They know that the suffering in this world can lead to intimacy
with You, because they have experienced this...

Truth

They know that time spent with You is the most important
thing to do

Truth

They know that the Holy Spirit is their encourager

Truth

The Holy Spirit gets them through

They have learned to thrive with Your joy in this life

Because they know it's all about Eternity

With You! The One who made it all!

I am no longer
afraid to be
seen and heard

Song of Vulnerability

I sing the Song of Vulnerability with my ideas, thoughts, and experiences. Knowing fully that I risk being misunderstood and disliked.

Vulnerability has often scared me. Being seen, heard, and real about my thoughts and feelings often came with unpleasant consequences. My voice was always small. I was so timid, especially as a child. While inside me, I yelled for freedom to be heard—to be vulnerable and real.

How would that really feel? "Real," in the sense of not being who others wanted me to be, not sure of my true identity. Then I met my Savior, Jesus, and He changed everything! My identity was now rooted in what He says about me.

So now I have learned to show up over and over being me. It is a risk worth taking. It's now okay not to always be understood or liked. So I sing the Song of Vulnerability.

It's okay if you don't like me

It's a risk worth taking

I am no longer afraid to be seen and heard

I now take a stand

The song of vulnerability

Sets me free

To be who I am in

Christ Jesus

And Him in me

My new identity

I sing the Song of Vulnerability

Showing up over and over being me

Christ in me

Will you join me in singing your

Song of Vulnerability?

With your new identity?

Christ in you

The One who sets you free...

To show up

And sing your Song

of Vulnerability

Vulnerability

157

Song of the Sand Dollar

I believe we all learn from someone. They shape our thoughts and passions for life. My mom loved to comb the seashore for hours looking for seashells and in particular, sand dollars. When she passed away, I was grieving her absence in my life. My mom was an overcomer and taught me many insights about living. One thing she taught me: spending time in nature can be very therapeutic. We also shared our love for Jesus and a passion for recovery. Both of us battled addiction issues and we are both very creative. My mom was special to me. Although we did not always agree, we found a way to be respectful to each other. I believe our shared faith helped our relationship. We could talk for hours about Jesus and how He helps us daily in our recovery. I appreciated her childlike faith and prayers. She talked to God like a child would. Those were precious times for me to remember.

I also have many difficult memories regarding my mom with her alcoholism and her mental health while growing up. But God in His grace gave my mom opportunity to be forgiven and to forgive. This is certainly the most beautiful legacy she passed onto me.

So I was at the beach one day, not long after her passing. I asked the Lord to please provide a sand dollar as I was thinking about my mom and all she had overcome with Christ. The Lord provided a sand dollar that day. I will never forget. So I sing the Song of the Sand Dollar.

Combing the beach one day

In memory of my mom

And remembering all she's overcome

She is now with her Savior, Jesus Christ

For all Eternity

I will see her again someday—

But her memory lives on and gives me peace

As I comb the beach

I ask the Lord, will You please provide

A sand dollar in memory of my sweet mom?

Then I look down and right in front of me

A sand dollar

All the memories of my mom come rushing in

Like the waves of the sea—

It overwhelms me

I remember my mom and

All she's overcome in Christ Jesus

Combing the beach that day, I will never forget

How God provided for me—

A sweet memory to keep

Now I overcome and Sing the Song

Of the Sand Dollar

I pray her legacy lives on

Song of Tears

As my tears begin to flow

I fear they will never stop

It's been too long since I have let them out

I pray they drip into my Father's hand

I pray He holds each one and never lets go

He tells me to let it all out—

You were never meant to carry all the burdens yourself

My Father knows me so well

I don't need to hide

I can let them all out

I can let the tears flow

For my Father knows how I feel, and He holds me close

He will never let me go

He reminds me that He feels my pain too

I am reminded that I am never alone

He calls me Beloved Child, as my tears drip into His

Heart

He holds me close

My Father knows I have experienced much loss

I know He understands

I give it to Him

I let it all out

I let the tears flow—

He knows me so well

I feel so much lighter now

I was holding them in too long

No longer afraid

No longer afraid

No longer afraid

Song of Sorrow

"In the morning when I rise, give me Jesus." These lyrics have become a song I cling to. The mornings can be difficult when grief settles in... loss—so deep it seems lile a heaviness that can't be explained. Saying the name of Jesus can break through this indescribable pain.

Psalm 34:18 says, "The Lord is near to the brokenhearted and saves the crushed in spirit." I believe this truth in Scripture. So I sing the Song of Sorrow.

So I fall to my knees and pray

Not even knowing what to say...

For my sorrow runs too deep

But the Lord sings the Song of Sorrow

For me to keep

It is only in His presence I find peace

It is only in His joy

That I find strength for today

It is only in His grace

That I find rest

It is only in His Word

It is only in His love

That I can sing the Song of Sorrow

I fall to my knees not knowing what to say

When my loss is overwhelming

But the Lord sings over me until it becomes

My song to sing

It is only in God's presence

I find peace

It is only in His joy I find strength

It is only in His grace I find rest

It is only in His Word

I find hope

It is only in His love

That I can sing the Song of Sorrow

Because God is close to the brokenhearted

I fall to my knees and pray, not knowing what to say

The grief is too much to bear

But the Lord in His grace sings over me

Oh child, now you know My Song of Sorrow

It is only in My presence

You will find

Peace, joy, and strength

It is only in My grace

You will find My rest, hope, and love

To sing My Song of Sorrow

So I fall to my knees and pray

I thank my Heavenly Father for

Sorrow

For only the brokenhearted can sing ...

The Song of Sorrow

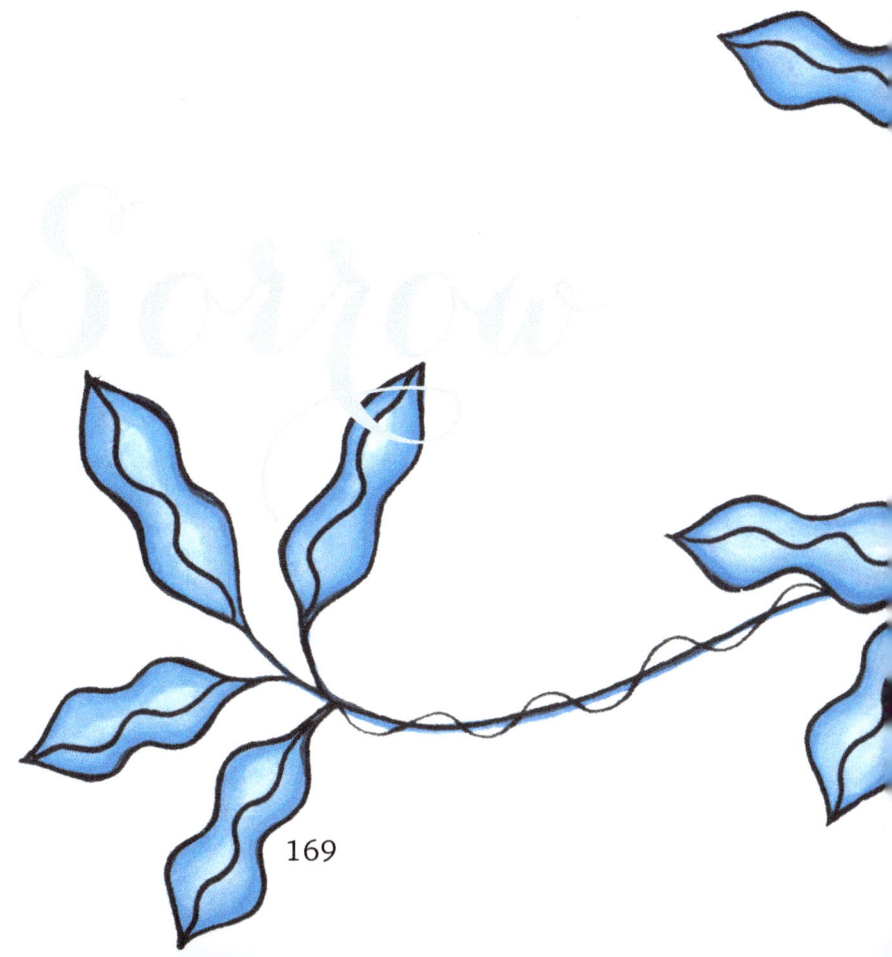

169

Song of Joy

Joy, oh Joy

Where have you escaped to?

It has been a while since you have embraced me

Then suddenly I remember where my Joy comes from—

It comes from You, LORD!

When I pray to You, LORD!

When I listen and obey You, LORD!

YOU are my Joy

YOU are my Strength

Joy, oh Joy

How I love Your embrace

How I love Your song

The Song of Joy on my lips—

LORD, you are My Joy and

My Strength!

You have not escaped

You are just waiting to be called upon

Oh, how I love Your Song of Joy on my lips

LORD, please embrace me with Your

JOY!

So I can sing the Song of Joy

So that others will remember where their Joy comes from...

It comes from You!

Only You, LORD

You are our Joy and our Strength!

Let My love
do its
work

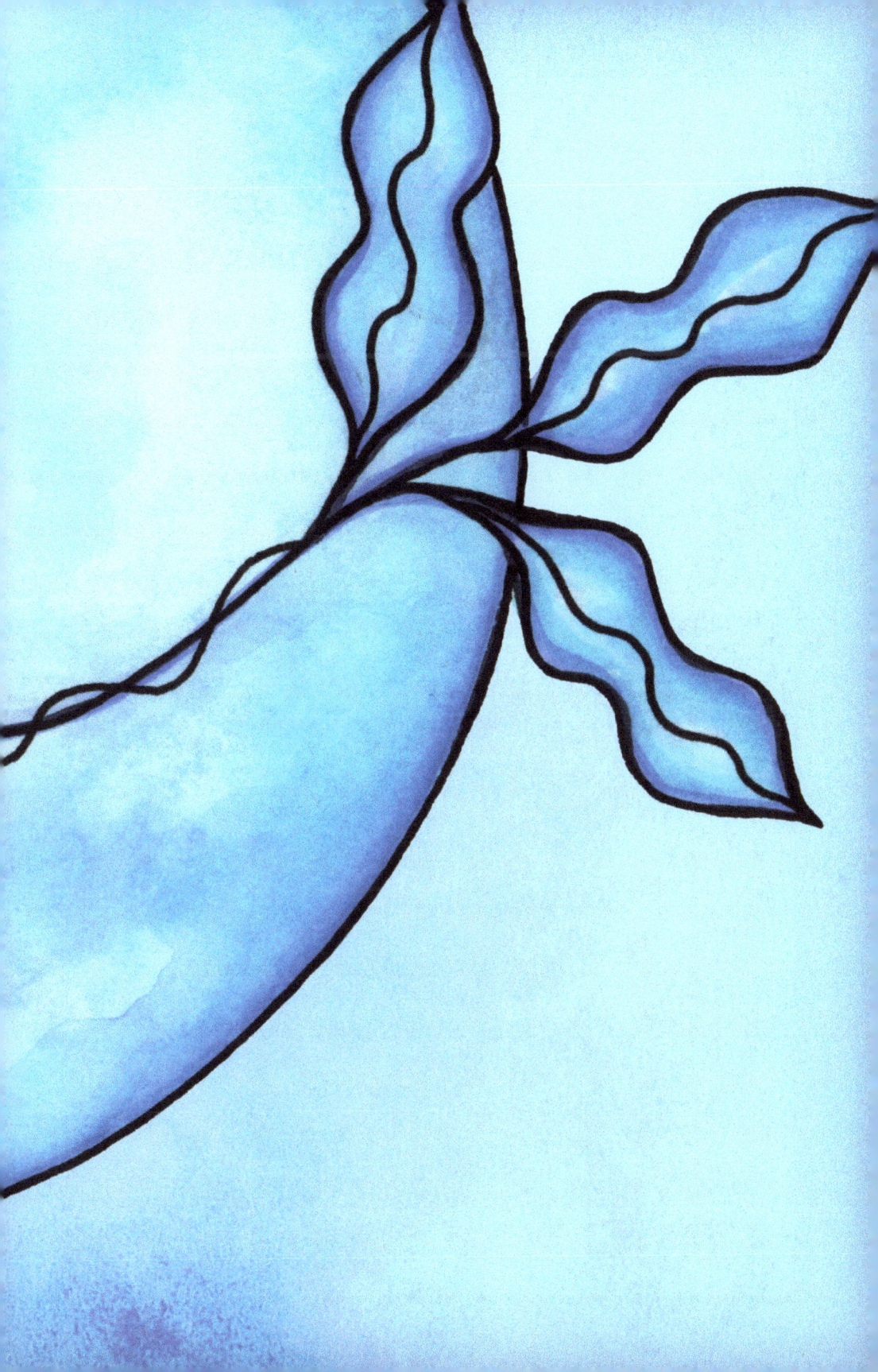

Song of Breaking

When my heart breaks in two

I cry out to You, Jesus

I know of nothing else to do

But I turn toward You, Jesus

You always show up when no one else will

When my heart breaks in two

You assure me that my heart will mend

You say wait and give it time

Let the forgiveness sink in

Let the bitterness go

Let God have HIS way

You assure me that my heart will mend

When my heart breaks in two

I turn toward You, Jesus... my friend

You always show up when no one else will

You say let My forgiveness sink in

Let My love do its work

YOU always assure me that my heart will mend

I turn toward You, Jesus, my friend

I give it time

I let the bitterness go

I let God have HIS way

I let the forgiveness sink in

I let Love do its work

My heart begins to mend

I sing the Song of Breaking

to You, Jesus, my trusted friend

You always show up

You always show up

You always show up

You say my heart will mend

When

I let God have HIS way!

177

Song of Healing

What I have learned about healing is that it comes in all forms, emotional, spiritual, and physcial. I have experienced them all in my lifetime at different stages and at different ages. What I have learned is that God is going to do only what God wants to do. So I sing the Song of Healing.

Lord, you are our Healer

You alone choose when and where

We can ask fervently in prayer

We can ask in faith and believe

But You still choose

When and where and how

Because You alone

Our Healer

YOU know what is best

Sometimes there is a test

Because You alone our

Creator

YOU know what is best

We can ask fervently in prayer

For ourselves and for another

We ask in faith and believe

We ask for YOUR will alone to be done

Lord, You are our Healer

And You choose when and where

The healing takes place

Because You are Father God

And You know what is best

Sometimes the waiting is the test

Sometimes the healing comes in rest

Sometimes our circumstances don't change

Sometimes healing comes in an instant

But as we ask fervently in prayer

We ask with faith and believe

We ask for Your will alone

What you are changing, Lord, is me!

What you are changing, Lord, is me!

As we rest, Lord, in the One who can do anything

HE chooses

As we rest in the One who can do anything!

181

Song of Recovery

I have had recovery from an eating disorder for over forty years, but some traumatic events entered my life unexpectedly—which led to grief, codependency, and sin.

I am grateful that I listened to God in prayer as I cried out to Him. He encouraged and reminded me about Celebrate Recovery. I have spent years helping others in their attempts to get help with their various hurts, habits, and hang-ups through a surrendered life with Jesus Christ. I know by my own experience that God knows we need Him, but we also thrive best in the right community. So I sing the Song of Recovery.

Oh the day I was brought to my knees

In recovery

O Lord, I confess

I have been trying once again to control my life and others

On my own

In my grief and sin

Oh, what a mess!

Can you please take my will and make it Yours?

I am brought to my knees in recovery

Please forgive me, Lord

I lay down my shame and guilt

I lay down the traumatic events

I lay down the hurt I have caused

I realize it's a lifelong process

One day at a time with You, Lord

So I fall to my knees and confess...

Lord, use me to bring others like me to enjoy

This journey

Of recovery

This journey of discovery

So I sing the Song of Recovery

Who knew my own song could help bring

Others along and confess that they need You, Lord

To take their will and make it Yours

And it's a lifelong process

This journey of recovery

This journey of discovery

This Song of Recovery that we can all share

As we sing together!

May we bring You glory, O Lord!

May we bring You glory, O Lord!

As we sing together!

Song of the Battle

The battle is on against good and evil—

Who will prevail?

Sometimes it's difficult to tell

Whose side are you on?

The Bible tells us in the end

Those who believe in You

Jesus…

Will stand

I can feel the evil ramping up

This is where we can't give in or give up!

It's no time to sleep

We must wake up!

The battle is real—

Every day a fight for your soul

Don't let evil take its toll

Turn to Jesus, Your Savior for

HE wins in the end

The battle is on against good and evil—

So please don't just blindly carry on

Wake up and see there is a path to choose...

Good or evil

Who will you follow to the end?

For Jesus wins in the end...

The battle is real against

Good and evil

So where do you stand?

There is no middle ground

Don't believe this lie

It's in Jesus' name where eternal life is found

It's in Jesus' name where eternal life is found!

Please choose this path and in the end

You will stand!

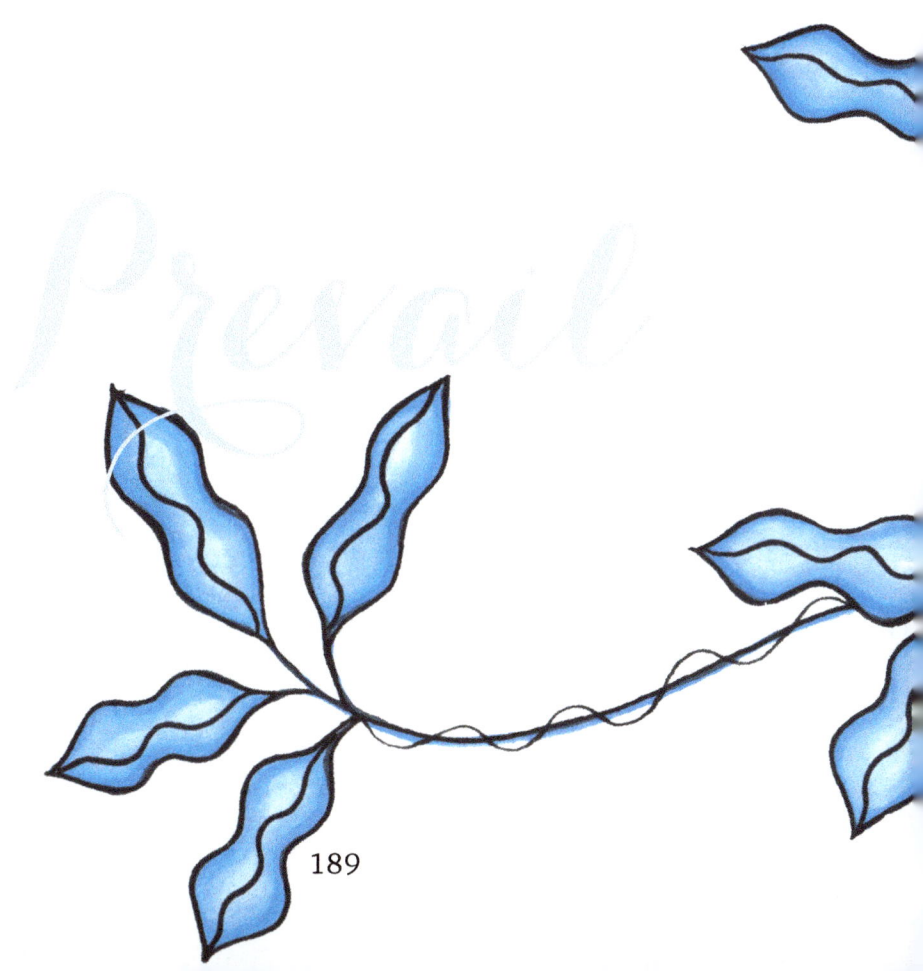

189

You, my
friend—
are the
Songbird!

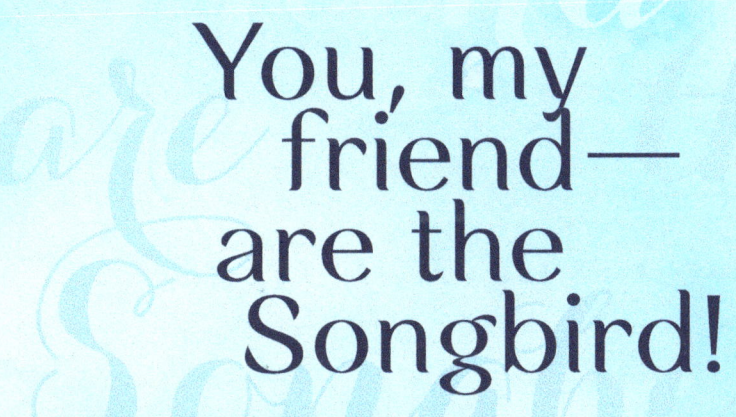

Songs in My Head

*E*ven when I was a young child, I knew there was someone watching over me—singing over me. I have always loved music. My brother who is five years older played the drums in his bedroom next to mine. I could hear the drumbeat as he practiced over and over to his favorite artists. Music became my friend and comfort. So I would have…

Songs in my Head

Drowning out the dread

The loud voices in my home

The midnight rage

I felt like a caged bird

Waiting to escape

So I would sing myself to sleep

But I always knew someone was watching over me

In the morning, I awake

A new day

Songs in My Head

A new day to pretend

That everything is okay

But I would drown out the dread

With the Songs in My Head

For so long I felt like a caged bird

Wanting to escape

So now I have learned to sing a new song

In the day that You have given me

In my darkness, in my dread—

I no longer pretend

For I learned it was You, Lord, all along watching over me—

Waiting for me to call on You

To set this Songbird free!

And now I am free indeed to sing the songs You have given me!

Song of My Little Songbird

My Little Songbird

Flew away

I know in my heart

God will make a way

To see her

Someday

And in the meantime

Just for today

I will remember the song she sang

To me

The sweetest melody

My Little Songbird

Flew away—

I know I will see her

Someday

And in the meantime

While I wait

God, please hold her close

As she makes her way

Just for today

I will pray

God, please keep my Little Songbird safe

As she grows and learns

I will always remember

The song she sang to me

The sweetest melody

My Little Songbird flew away

I know God will make a way

To see her

Someday

And in the waiting

Please, God, draw her close to You

Like only You can do

I trust You, Lord, with my Little Songbird

I know, God, You will make a way

To see her

Someday

My Little Songbird

Will have a new song to sing

And it will be a sweet melody

She will sing Your song

So I pray

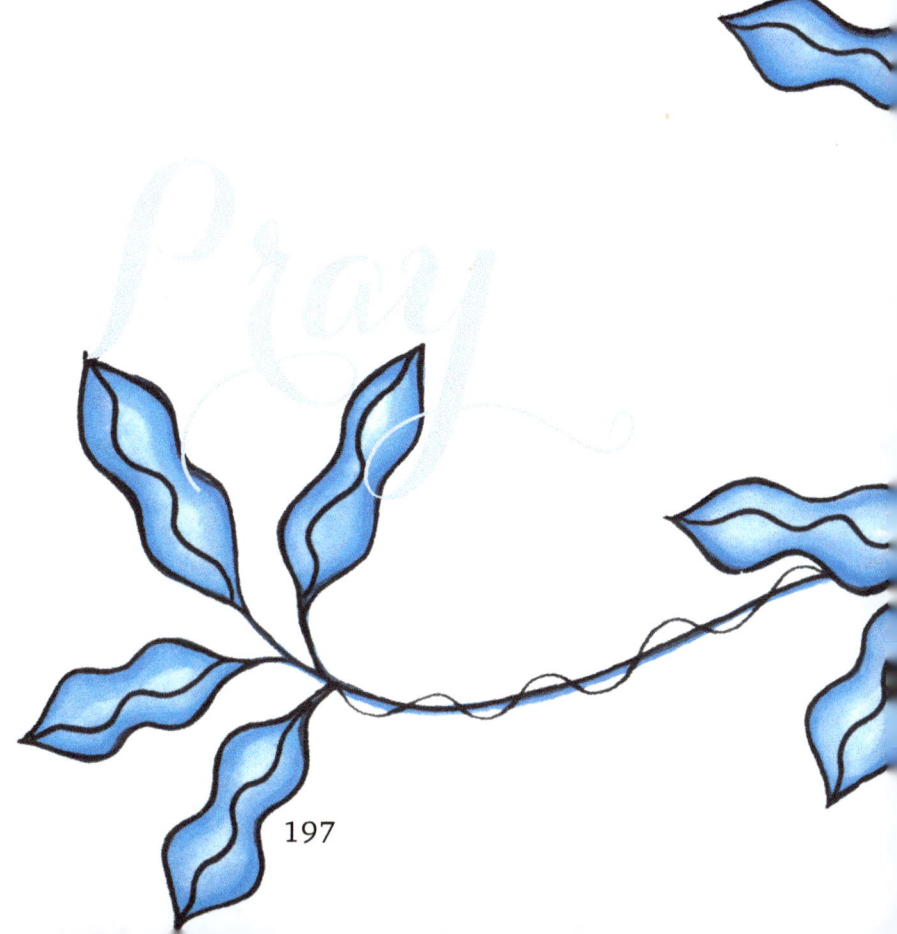

God, you
made a way.
My Little
Songbird flew
back to me.
Oh, what a
day!

Song of Flying Home

My Little Songbird flew back to me!

I knew in my heart

God would make a way

My longing heart was met today

My fervent prayers were answered

In God's time

In God's way

My Little Songbird flew back to me

My sorrow turned to joy

You, O Lord, kept my Songbird safe

While I waited, prayed, and anticipated

To hear her new song

As You promised You would

You kept her close

You made a way

You helped her learn and grow

You taught her a new song to sing!

The sweetest melody

My Little Songbird flew back to me

Singing Your song

Singing Your song

Now she is teaching me

Song of He's Alive

I remember when my daughter came rushing into our bedroom very early one Easter morning. She was so excited she could not contain herself. She had to tell us, "Jesus is alive—He is no longer dead!"

My daughter at only three had songs in her little head. Always singing... I loved hearing her. I still do. She could carry a tune. I not so much, but I love music, and worship music was and still is a significant part of our daily lives. Music connects people and has a way of breaking through barriers.

So today I sing the Song of He's Alive!

He's alive!

He's alive!

He is no longer dead

This is the song in my daughter's head

That Easter morning, I will never forget

She knew in her heart with childlike faith

That Jesus Christ had risen from the grave

That Jesus Christ could save us from our sin

If we believe in HIM

Put our trust in HIM

So she sings

With great confidence

And she's been singing ever since,

With that childlike faith

He's alive!

He's alive!

He's no longer dead!

I will never forget—

He's alive!

He's alive!

He is no longer dead!

He will come back again!

And she's been singing ever since

Song of It's Not About Me

Over the many years of having the privilege of studying the life and ministry of Jesus Christ, I have come to the conclusion from my own experiences with God that it is about conforming to the image of Jesus Christ, my Savior and LORD. So I sing the Song of It's Not About Me.

It's all about You, Jesus

Less of me, more of You, Jesus

Dying to myself

Conforming to Your image

It's all about You, Jesus

Will You show me how to serve

So it's less about me and more about You?

You, Jesus, take the towel

And wash the feet

You feed the poor

And those in need

You heal the sick

And mend the brokenhearted

You share the good news and forgiveness of sin

You promise eternal life to those who believe on Your name

You died, were buried,

And You rose from the dead

For our sins—

It's all about You, Jesus

You have shown me Your way

So it's all about You, Jesus

Less about me

More about You

Jesus, You have shown me how to serve

From Your Word—

So will I obey?

It's not about me, it's all about You

So I take a towel

And wash the feet

I feed the poor

And those in need

I comfort the sick

And mend the brokenhearted in Your name

I share the good news of eternal life

About You, Jesus

You died, were buried, and rose from the grave

For our sins

Jesus, You have shown me the way

It's not about me

Dying to myself

Conforming to Your image

I daily seek

More of You

Less of me

I pray

Conforming to Your image

Until the day I see You face to face

Song of Serenity

Lord, I am in a place today where I have nothing to prove

I think it's where You can finally

Move

In me

And through me

I am free

I have nothing to prove

Today

Lord, You can move

Freely in me

All my longings are in

You

You say to live for

Today

And it's what I will

Do

I have nothing to prove

I belong to You

I think it's where You can finally move

In me

And through me

I am free

In You

And You

In me

I am free

In You

And You

In me

211

Song of the Master

Christ is "All and in All"

Christ is All in the work of salvation

Yours and mine

For all time

Christ is All in the work of redemption

Saving us from our sin—

For all time

Christ is All in the work of your purpose

Granting gifts by His grace to you and me—

For all time

Christ is All and in All

Master

Savior

King

for all eternity

Christ is All and in All

Master

Savior

King

Christ is All and in All

And dwells in you and me!

We are HIS temple and His

Glory shines through

Christ is All and in All for you and me

Master, Savior, King

Worthy of all worship

For All Eternity

Inspired by Colossians 3:11

Song of Surprise

You came into my life like a big surprise

But it wasn't a surprise to You—

You have always had Your eye on me

Before I knew Your name

You were there

But You have always been there

Singing over me

You came into my life like a big

Surprise

You have opened my eyes

I see life so differently

The love You have for me is so real

The joy You feel for me is overwhelming

The grace You pour on me in my suffering

It is hard to describe

But I will sing my Song of Surprise to You

My Lord

You came into my life like a big surprise—

But it wasn't to You…

You have always had Your eye on me

The hope You give is so real

The peace in Your presence that I can feel

The patience You have for me

The mercy I don't deserve

It is hard to describe—

But I want others to understand

That You are real!

So I will continue to sing my Song of Surprise

For the day I called Your name and believed

I have never been the same

I have never been the same

The day You came into my life!

Like a big surprise

But it wasn't to You!

I have always been on Your mind

Now You are on my mind

Now You are on my mind

Song of Imagine

I can't imagine my life without You, LORD

Everything I do I long to glorify You

What would my purpose be if I couldn't worship You

My songs would be empty

My life would have no meaning

Because everything I want to do is wrapped up

In my love for You, LORD

I can't imagine my life without You, LORD

Everything I do, I long to glorify YOU

You are my Father and my Friend

You know my beginning and my end

and everything in between

You still love me…

It's hard to comprehend

What purpose would I have if I couldn't worship You?

My songs would be empty

My life would have no meaning

Because everything I want to do is wrapped up

In my love for You, O LORD

Song of Love

Your love, Jesus, compels me

to see everything so differently

Your love, Jesus, grips me

To hold everything in this world loosely

As I wait for Your coming

I sit quietly in the love You have for me

And it compels me

I see the brokenness in the woman's eyes

As she cries

I see the heartache behind the smile

As a man mourns his wayward child

Your love, Jesus, compels me

To see everything

So differently

Your love grips me

To hold everything in this world loosely

I now let go of what I can't control

You, Jesus, are powerful

You, Jesus, are powerful

I see Your hand on everything

There's nothing You can't touch

I see the marriage where they are about to give up

I see the addict who's had enough

I see the one who suffered abuse

I see the teen trying to fit in

And as they cry out to You

There's nothing You can't touch

I've seen miracles

I see Your hand on everything

I see the one who has everything the world has to give

Trapped in their mind of misery

The one who looks in the mirror and only sees her flaws

And that's her identity

But I believe in Jesus

And there's nothing He can't touch

I see His hand on everything

I've seen His hand on me

I've seen His hand on you

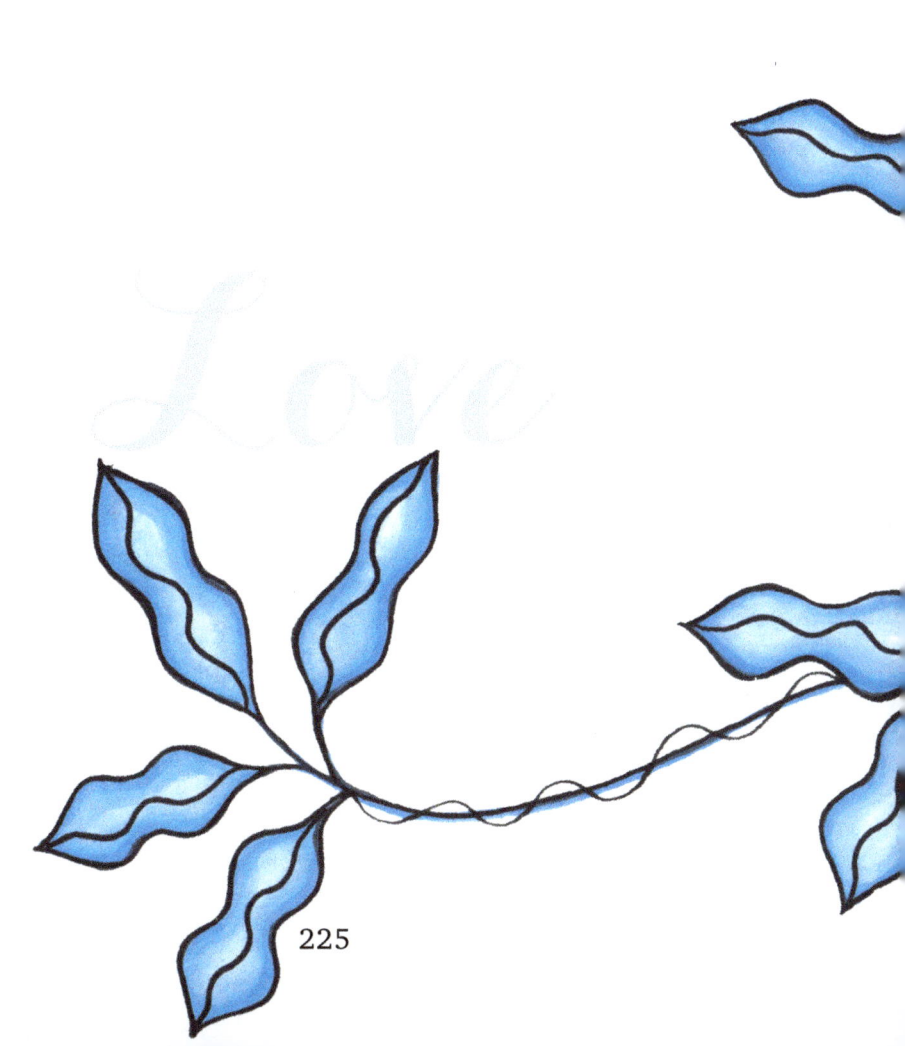

Song of Ascend

I often picture in my mind that Jesus Christ is climbing stairs and he is reaching down to me with his right hand. It is like He is saying come up with me—ascend... to higher heights. So I sing the Song of Ascend.

As Jesus climbs the stairs

He reaches down

He offers His hand

He smiles lovingly

I reach up

I take His hand

With childlike faith

I smile back

We ascend

One step at a time

To higher heights

I don't know what's around the bend

So I sing the Song of Ascend …

We climb together

Hand in hand

Jesus is my forever friend …

He doesn't let go

Even when my fears creep in

Even when I doubt what is next

Even when there is a test

Even when I can't in my own strength take another step

He reminds me of who holds my hand—

The One who endured the cross

For our sins …

The One who has victory over even death

So we ascend together

To new levels

To higher heights

One step at a time

Together

I get excited

I pass the test

We ascend together

He doesn't let go

Jesus my forever friend

Jesus is reaching out to you ... today

So you can sing the Song of Ascend

Ascend

Song of the Baton

What do we do with the baton in a relay race?

The goal is to pass it on in a way that it doesn't get dropped, but also to not lose momentum in the race.

I enjoyed a sweet friendship with a beautiful older woman who taught me many valuable principles through her Godly example and by her carefully chosen words. We were able to serve in Bible study together for many years. She had a genuine passion and calling to disciple women one-on-one. She inspired me to see my life in the same way. I will never forget her words—she said, "I want to disciple women until I take my last breath." Years later, she passed away doing just that. The Lord took her home in between her discipleship appointments.

At her memorial service, batons were passed out in her honor with 2 Timothy 2:2 inscribed on them.
I still have the baton.

It is a reminder of her and my calling. So I sing the

Song of the Baton.

O Lord, my desire is to pass on the baton

In spirit and in truth

To those whose greatest desire is to follow after You—

Those who are trustworthy with Your Word

Able to pass on to others

The truths they have learned

Without losing momentum

Disciples of Christ

Following Your way

In this race called life—

Focused on passing on the baton

YOU, Jesus, are the Baton we are passing on—

Our relationship with You

YOU are the Baton we want to carry on—

To the next generation

YOU alone are the Way, the Truth, and the Life

The only way to the Father

Disciples of Christ

Following Your way...

In this race called life

Passing YOUR truth onto the next generation

Holy Spirit, help us to not lose momentum

YOU, Jesus, are the Baton we are passing on

May I be found speaking in spirit and in truth

To those who are trustworthy with Your Word

And when I pass from this life into the next

When I take my last breath

Then

I will see YOU Jesus, the Baton

And all Your disciples, who passed it on

Disciples of

Jesus Christ

Together

For all eternity

Singing the Song of the Baton!

233

Acknowledgements

My heartfelt thanks goes to my gifted and beautiful daughter, Kadie Schaefer, for creating the perfect artwork for this book. Thank you, Kadie, for listening, encouraging, and inspiring me with my vision. You are my cheerleader! Your artwork paired with my poetry is an expression of our creativity and the love we share in our deep relationship with Jesus and one another.

I want to thank my husband, Steve, for being a strong example to me of perseverance under trials. Our shared faith in Jesus Christ helps us to grow together, but also individually, as we encourage one another. Thank you for your daily prayers and gracious support in my healing journey writing this book.

Holly DelHousaye, my gracious mentor, dear friend, and confidant—thank you for believing in me, challenging me, and speaking life into me during some dark times. Thank you for reading through some poems in the very beginning and encouraging me to keep writing. You would say, "Writing is a process, take your time... it's like giving birth." Holly, thank you for reminding me to consecrate all I do unto the Lord and for being a consistent voice in my life who speaks the truth in love from an eternal perspective.

Naomi Rhode came into my life when I was grieving the sudden loss of my mom and then the loss of my dad. Thank you Naomi for being a precious friend, mentor, and a mother figure to me. As we started meeting and I shared my vision about the *Songbird* book and a few poems, she said, "Do it— I love it!" Naomi is a faithful encourager, and guides me with words that penetrate my soul.

I want to thank my gifted new friend Sara Lin for her creative direction, her encouragement, and knowledgeable skills in helping me bring this book to the finish line.

Thank you, Cindy Goodman, for pouring gently into my life as a minister of God's grace. You helped create a safe space to be vulnerable when I showed up over four years ago to Celebrate Recovery. I am grateful to God for your friendship and that we can be fellow Songbirds-in-training.

I want to thank my recovery community for sharing together in our hurts, hang-ups, and habits through our shared personal testimonies, our friendships, and our shared accountability. It is truly beyond inspiring to see what God can do with a surrendered life in Jesus Christ, as we each take steps through our process of being sanctified.

"Be still and know that I am God."

PSALM 46:10

Did you know songbirds learn to sing in the dark? They hear the song from their fathers and start warbling the pattern from the VERY beginning. What they learn in the dark, they sing in the day. This collection of poetry is a vulnerable and ongoing conversation with the Heavenly Father. The author finds joy in her "nights" as she learns from the One who taught the birds to sing. Readers can relate to her struggles; her honest and unpretentious connection with God evokes a modern-day book of Psalms. *Songbirds Learn to Sing in the Dark* is a love song to the Savior—for all who call on His name and wait breathlessly to hear His voice.

 **ABOUT TRACY** Tracy Fedyski's journey as a grateful believer in Jesus Christ, wife, mother, grandmother, friend, mentor, business owner, Bible teacher, and her involvement in the recovery community has given her insight and unique opportunities only God could have orchestrated. *Songbirds Learn to Sing in the Dark* is Tracy's poetically penned testimony of learning to listen to God's voice in the dark... in the stillness and silence... in the valleys of life. She emerges out of darkness with a song to sing in the day. Tracy resides in sunny Scottsdale, Arizona and has been married to her husband, Steve, for forty-two years. They have two adult children and six grandchildren that keep them quite active.

"Every poem hums with the healing cadence of a woman who has learned to let grief be a tutor and joy be her anthem. Through Tracy's gift, the Holy Spirit gets to hold the pen. The result? A chorus of truth, grace, and sacred encouragement. This is not just a book—it's a tender call back to the Voice that first spoke love into us. So, if your heart has ever limped through the valley or longed for the morning, let *Songbird* be the lantern you carry. Tracy's song is strong, Spirit-led, and gently unforgettable."

—Cindy Goodman
Minister, Recovery Advocate, and Fellow Songbird-in-Training

ISBN 979-8-9925756-2-0

www.ingramcontent.com/pod-product-compliance
Lightning Source LLC
Chambersburg PA
CBHW051612120626
46551CB00014B/1764